Deconstructing Terrorist Violence

Deconstructing Terrorist Violence

Faith as a Mask

Ram Puniyani

⑤SAGE www.sagepublications.com
Los Angeles • London • New Delhi • Singapore • Washington DC • Boston

First published in 2015 by

SAGE Publications India Pvt Ltd
B1/I-1 Mohan Cooperative Industrial Area
Mathura Road, New Delhi 110 044, India
www.sagepub.in

SAGE Publications Inc
2455 Teller Road
Thousand Oaks, California 91320, USA

SAGE Publications Ltd
1 Oliver's Yard, 55 City Road
London EC1Y 1SP, United Kingdom

SAGE Publications Asia-Pacific Pte Ltd
3 Church Street
#10-04 Samsung Hub
Singapore 049483

Published by Vivek Mehra for SAGE Publications India Pvt Ltd, typeset in 10/13 Berkeley by RECTO Graphics, Delhi, and printed at Chaman Enterprises, New Delhi.

Library of Congress Cataloging-in-Publication Data Available

ISBN: 978-93-515-0064-3 (HB)

The SAGE Team: Rudra Narayan, Neha Sharma, Mriga Maithel, Anju Saxena, and Rajinder Kaur

Contents

Preface:

A World Gripped by Terror: Is Terrorism Due to Religion?

The last few decades have seen many attacks of terror, more so after the ghastly tragedy of 9/11, 2001. Immediately after the 9/11 tragedy, the US media coined a phrase, 'Islamic Terrorism'. Since then, many formulations have been derived from this phrase, like 'All terrorists are Muslims', and have become part of popular perception and the guiding light of policy-makers and investigating agencies. After every act of terror, some Muslim terror groups' names are floated and action planned. In India, in particular, after most of the acts of terror during the period from 2004 till 2012, in the aftermath of the terror tragedies, the Muslim youth were arrested in large numbers. Most of them had to be released due to the lack of any credible evidence. The impact of this formulation was created by the media of the United States, picked up by others, and propagated by various organizations and people, and had immense impact on the popular psyche all over the world. Later, we saw with the association of Sadhvi Pragya Singh Thakur and Swami Aseemanand the acts of terror that came to be known as Saffron terror or Hindutva terror.

After all, what is terrorism? Is it due to religion and religious community, or due to politics? Popularly, it is being associated with religion, 'Islamic terrorism', or 'Hindutva terrorism'. Hindutva, anyway, gives the impression of being a religion, but it is politics. As such, it is difficult to define terrorism, as some people whom we regard as terrorists may be regarded as freedom fighters by others.

Terrorism is different from communal violence. In communal violence, one communal group spreads hatred against the other community, and average layers of society are mobilized to attack minority groups.

Sometimes, two religious communities are also pitted against each other. The Gujarat carnage (2002), the Mumbai violence (1992), and the Orissa violence (2008) fall in this category. Terrorism is planned secretly, and its execution comes as a surprise; communal violence is built up and its perpetrators are easy to locate. In the case of the Mumbai violence, an intense hate atmosphere against minorities was built up by a section of the media and by word of mouth, and then average people were made to believe that minorities are a threat to them and so they should be attacked. In Mumbai, it happened in the wake of the Babri demolition, and in Gujarat, it happened after the Godhra train burning. Simply speaking, in the latter case, those guilty of the train burning should have been punished, but an atmosphere was created against the whole community and poor sections of Hindus were mobilized to attack Muslims.

In Orissa and many parts of the country, there is a make-believe perception that Christian missionaries are converting by force and fraud is the popular mind set. As such, if we see, there is not a single case in the police record where a complaint against missionaries for conversion has been registered. Christianity is one of the oldest religions of India, and today the population of Christians is a mere 2.3 percent of the country's entire population. This population of Christians has been on a decline, from 2.6 percent in 1971 to 2.3 percent in 2001. The Wadhva Commission report, which went into the killing of Pastor Graham Stains in 1999, showed that the Pastor was not involved in acts of conversion and that the Christian population in his area of work was fairly stable. This perception about missionary work has been used to instigate violence against a tiny minority of the country.

As such, terrorism is due to social, economic, and political reasons, and terrorists have come from all religions. Let us recall the killers of Mahatma Gandhi, Indira Gandhi, and Rajiv Gandhi. Similarly, a one-time biggest terrorist organization was the Liberation Tigers of Tamil Elam (LTTE). The Irish Republican Army constituted mainly by Christians has been indulging in acts of terror in Ireland for a long time. Just a couple of years ago, a Christian Norwegian youth, Anders Berling Brevik, killed 86 youths.

No one is a born terrorist. Some youths take to the path of terror due to gross injustice or the perception of injustice done to them or their community. This is associated with a feeling that the society state will not give them justice. There is another reason for terrorism, and that pertains to the political goals of dominant nations or dominant groups, such as the desire for control over oil wealth by the United States. The other major cause of terrorism is ethno-national, as in the case of Jaffna, Sri Lanka, where the LTTE gained power Kashmir, where the issue of autonomy became an ethno-national one, and the Northeast, where Northeast's integration into Indian mainstream gave the hiccups of terrorism. Similarly, the IRA was also formed due to ethnic injustices.

We are also witnessing the involvement of some Hindutva elements, such as Sadhvi Pragya Singh Thakur, Swami Aseemanand, and others, in the acts of terror related to the blasts in front of the mosques in Malegaon, the Ajmer Dargah, the Samjhauta Express, etc. This again is due to the indoctrination of the minds of the people by the political process, by ideologies which are totally antidemocratic and look at politics in the colors of religion. Here, the minds of the people have been indoctrinated with the belief that a particular community is under threat due to another community. One knows that the threat is not due to a religious community, but since this politics is based on communal principles, they attribute all the reasons to religion and so the misconception is deliberately produced, resulting in violence.

The type of terrorism that we witnessed in Mumbai (November 2008) is the leftover of the indoctrinated Al Qaeda-type groups. Let us remember that once a person is indoctrinated for political goals, the reversal of such a process is practically impossible. Today, the country is a victim of this insane process, which has been the result of various global and local political and economic processes. We need to look beyond the symptoms of terrorism and understand the disease that is infesting our social fabric.

The primary focus of this book is to understand that terrorism is a phenomenon driven by political, social, and economic agendas. The major roots of terrorism today are hidden in the agenda of control over oil resources by the United States. In India, terrorism has its roots in the fallout of India -Pakistan relations, and Hindutva politics. We need to see that associating a political–economic phenomenon with religion has caused great damage to the religious community so targeted and has been the cause of intercommunity discord. In India, the groups acting in the name of Islam have been made accountable for most acts of terror, and the groups emerging from the Hindutva ideology who have been very active and have indulged in various acts of terror have been labeled as Hindu terrorists. Both ways, the identity of religion is abused for goals which have nothing to do with religion.

Since religion is being used as a cover, a mask for political goals, it incites many hysterical reactions against one or the other religious community. The political agenda and goals hide behind the identity of religion, which makes fighting against terrorism much more difficult. This book is an attempt to uncover the layers of religion to unravel the underlying politics. That is how it delves into the phenomenon of religion and also engages with global issues, where religion is tagged with this politics. There are many aspects of the phenomenon of terror; its popular perception as being due to religion is a very dangerous one. The main focus of the book is to try to show that terrorism is a political phenomenon, either aiming to control the oil-rich areas or having an agenda of sectarian nationalism. The book begins with a description of the acts of terror and their analysis and then goes on to show that the particular religion which is being implicated has nothing whatsoever to do with these acts of terror. The book aims to deconstruct the phenomenon of terrorism and shows that faith is being used as a mask for this deadly phenomenon.

Introduction:

The Politics of Terror in Contemporary Times

The current times are full of insane acts of terror. All over the globe as well as in India, acts of violence by political groups seeking justice or revenge are a dime a dozen. 9/11, 2001, brought to the fore this dreaded phenomenon, attracting global attention. In this attack, over 3,000 innocent people died. Later, many terror attacks were witnessed in Pakistan, India, Afghanistan, and other places. Not a month passes when one does not hear about the death of innocents in one more such act in some corner of the globe.

Tragically, India has been witnessing these acts of terror for a very long time.

> These acts have occurred more so from last two decades, to be precise after the Mumbai Carnage of 1992–93 and later have been occurring at regular intervals in different cities. There is a long list of these tragic acts but some of these which have tormented the society and are permanently etched in our memory are, March 1993: Mumbai serial bombings, which killed 257 people and injured more than 1,100, December 13th, 2001. (Puniyani 2009)

A few of these terror attacks are the following. On December 13, 2001, more than a dozen people, including five gunmen, were killed in an attack on the Parliament in New Delhi. On May 14, 2002, militants attacked an army camp near Kashmir's winter capital, Jammu, killing more than 30, including wives and children of soldiers. On September 24, 2002, militants with guns and explosives attacked the Hindu Akshardham temple in the western state of Gujarat, killing 31 and injuring more than 80.

In August 2003, two taxis packed with explosives blew up outside a Mumbai tourist attraction and a busy market, killing 52 and wounding more than 100. In October 2005, three bombs placed in busy New Delhi markets killed 62 people and injured hundreds. In March 2006, twin bombings at a train station and the Sankatmochan temple in Varanasi killed 20 people.

In July 2006, seven bombs on Mumbai's trains killed over 200 people and injured 700 others. On September 8, 2006, twin blasts at a mosque in Malegaon killed 30 and injured 100. On February 19, 2007, two bombs exploded aboard a train from India to Pakistan, the Samjhauta Express, burning to death at least 66 passengers; most of them were Pakistanis. On May 18, 2007, a bomb exploded during Friday prayers at a historic mosque, Mecca Masjid, Hyderabad, killing 14 people, of which five died in the police firing later. The police later shot dead five people in clashes with hundreds of enraged Muslims who protested against the attack. On August 25, 2007, three explosions a few minutes apart at an amusement park and a street-side food stall in Hyderabad killed 40 people. On May 13, 2008, seven blasts hit Jaipur, killing at least 63 people and wounding hundreds. On July 25, 2008, nine explosions in Bangalore caused terror, killing two people and injuring 12. On July 26, 2008, 21 blasts hit Ahmedabad, killing 55 and injuring 100. Meanwhile, 24 live bombs were claimed to have been recovered from Surat. On September 13, 2008, five blasts rocked the busy markets of New Delhi, killing 25 and injuring over 100, and three live bombs were defused at India Gate, Regal Cinema, and Central Park, respectively.

The picture could not have been worse at any point of time. The impact of terrorism on the lives of people has been felt all over the world, affecting their social life to a great extent. Security has been tightened at airports all across the globe. Huge forces have been deployed at airports to check and cross-check passengers. People have become used to being frisked and searched during travels. Muslims have borne the biggest brunt of these searches. Just being a Muslim is enough cause for someone to be thoroughly probed and searched. In the wake of the Mumbai blasts, the wholesale arrest of Muslim youths has been the norm with the police. The grounds for arrest that are cited are that they must be harboring terrorists, and that they must be having sympathies with terrorists since they are Muslims. Social life too is being affected in an adverse manner. The orthodoxy and right-wing religiopolitical streams are coming to the fore in a very aggressive and assertive manner. To top it all, some messages have been filtered down the social conduits, the ones related to Muslims and Islam, propagating that they are the fountainhead of violence and terror. Along with this, the sense of insecurity amongst average people is rising and some political elements are playing on this to increase their political clout. The atmosphere is full of suspicion. To worsen matters, there is a section of global and local media playing on this sentiment to widen the divide between different religious communities. There are sectarian groups, wearing different garbs, which are having a field day in reaping the harvest of hate.

Defining Terrorism

Defining terrorism is not very simple; various interpretations and definitions of terrorism have come up in recent times. The states have focused on talking about terrorist acts and violence, and deaths of innocents in this process. As such, in popular parlance, in some regions and circles, these acts of terror are legitimized as acts of political campaign. In these sections, the LTTE, the United Liberation Front of Assam (ULFA), the IRA, and Kashmiri militants, who are labeled as terrorists, are looked up to as freedom fighters. As such, terrorism can be understood "as an act of violence against unarmed civilians as a means of bargaining politically over specific demands or making a general statement" (Hensman 2002, 29). Further, Hensman adds very aptly, "It should be irrelevant whether the perpetrators are state parties or nonstate parties, and other characteristics (like skin color, ethnicity, gender, religion, nationality, sexual orientation, disability, social origin or anything else) of the perpetrators or the victims should likewise be irrelevant" (ibid., 156). While such groups have wreaked havoc, even the elected governments have resorted to violence.

> Statist definitions (*of terrorism*) portray terrorism to cover sedition, conspiracy, killing, murder, arson, explosions and public disorder to undermine the state…, twist due process of and evidentiary norms against the individual and prescribe heavy punishment…political terrorism abjures the state's definition and seeks to define terrorism as political freedom struggle to support the claims of justice and self-determination with no holds barred. (Dhavan 2006)

Accordingly, state governments formulate harsh laws and try to go overboard in their response to the extent of punishing the innocents in the process, resulting in the formulation of acts such as the War on Terror, Prevention of Terrorism Act (POTA), and armed forces acts. Dhavan further adds, "A people's definition of terrorism draws from the experience of civilian populations. Post World War II (WW II), terrorism against the people acquired a new dimension when America bombed Hiroshima and Nagasaki in 1945 and later carpet bombed Vietnam with Napalm." The experience of Afghanistan and Iraq is no different, nor is the one of Israel's attack on Lebanon.

Islam, Muslims, and Terrorism

The perception prevalent in the aftermath of 9/11, 2001, has been that terrorism is a result of the teachings of Islam and is carried out by Muslims. After the 9/11, 2001 attack on the World Trade Center (WTC), the term 'Islamic terrorism' started being popularized, and by now it has become part of social common sense.

> In India, the Kashmir militancy indulged in by a section of youth is again cited as example of Muslim terrorists. To add to this the incidents of Akshardham temple, 26/11, 2008 Mumbai attack, Ansal Plaza, hijacking of Indian Airlines plane to Kandhar, attack on parliament are blown up as, in all these either Muslims were involved or in some cases it was projected that they were. Some of these report had serious holes in the story presented by the authorities, but since there can be no ratification by citizens committees it is difficult to doubt or believe in some of these. (Puniyani 2010, 15)

All said and done, there are enough number of cases where Muslims are involved, and organizations such as Al Qaeda, Lashkar-e-Taiba, and Hamas have become names known in every household. But interestingly, there are many other organizations using violence which are not much taken note of.

Terrorists as such have come from many religions. But they have not resorted to this path due to religion. One such major organization was the LTTE, a militant group the majority of the members of which were Hindus. One member of this group, Dhanu, was the suicide bomber who killed Rajiv Gandhi. Similarly, the Khalistani movement was the major force resorting to terror just few years ago. Militants belonging to Christianity and Hinduism are active in Northeast India.

IRA militants worldwide belong to Christianity; the one who bombed a hotel in Cairo in 1942 was a Jew, and the Oklahoma bomber, Timothy McWeigh, was a Christian. Over 80 youth campers were killed in a shooting spree by Anders Behring Breivik, also a Christian (http://articles.nydailynews.com/2011-07-24/news/29827213_1_summer-camp-cold-blooded-killer-shot [last accessed on October 10, 2014]). Wherever dissatisfaction goes beyond a particular level, some of the people do resort to violence to achieve their supposed goal. It is not related to any one religion in particular. The National Democratic Front: Bodoland, All Tripura Tiger Force, Japanese Red Army, Lords Salvation Army, and Euskadi Ta Askatasuna (ETA), Spain, are some more examples of organizations which are scattered in different parts of world, using terror tactics for their political goals and having nothing to do with Islam.

During the last decade-and-a-half, Islam has been propagated to be a violent religion. The media and many political groups have projected this image of Islam on purpose. As such, Muslims are no uniform community. The basic assumption which comes from this formulation is that religion is the cause of terrorism. On the contrary, terrorism is a phenomenon which comes into being due to social, political, and economic circumstances. Religion is used as a cover for terrorist activities. The identity of terrorists is not always derived from and is not always centered around religion. As such, Khalistanis derived their identity from Sikhism. The alleged Muslim terrorists had multiple identities; the ones in Palestine, from where terrorism began, had Palestinian identity, and in Kashmir, it began as *Kashmiriyat* (Kashmirhood). The Islamic identity with this sort of terrorism came more particularly with Al Qaeda, which was set up by the Central Intelligence Agency (CIA), the United States, through the Inter-Services Intelligence (ISI) of Pakistan to fight against the USSR (Union of Soviet Socialist Republics) armies in Afghanistan.

Terrorism and Religion's Identity

It is true that some terrorists exhibit their Islamic identity, but that is not true always. Khalistanis also operated under the Sikh identity. There is a large variations in interpretation of Islam. The one's trained in the CIA sponsored Madrassas asserted that their interpretation of *the* Islam is the right one and they did the killings and called this action as jihad.

Those killed were called kafirs. As such they were indoctrinated in the madrassas especially set up for this purpose by the CIA. These madrassas were set up under the Kissinger doctrine of 'Asians should be made to fight Asians'. It was taught in the madrassas that the communists are *kafirs* (one who hides truth) since they do not believe in Allah, and killing them is *jihad*, and those dying in this *jihad* will go straight to *jannat* (heaven), where 72 virgins are waiting for them. This concoction of the US set-up madrassas had a strong impact on the Muslim youth who came in to get training in these with the readiness to lay down their lives for the US goal of occupying Afghanistan in the long run. This was clear in the way Al Qaeda members were treated in the White House (http://www.informationclearinghouse.info/article9561.htm [last accessed on October 10, 2014]). What is the so-called Islamic identity of terrorists? Only those trained in madrassas, set up by the CIA–ISI nexus, use the Islamic identity. In this violence words jihad and kafir were used.

What the madrassas set up by the CIA–ISI did was a very clever manipulation of words like *jihad* and *kafir* in particular. As we know, the historical meaning of these terms was much different in the beginning. Also, there are many interpretations of these words. And there are different interpretations of Islam. The media highlights any sensational violent act and ignores the pacifist ones. Comments of fanatics are projected prominently as the Islamic voice. The sober and moderate statements are either ignored or find their place in some small corner of the media.

The misuse of the word *jihad* by fanatics adds to the problem. Any act of Muslim terrorists is supposed to be a *jihad*, as some of them project it in the same manner. As such, the holywar crusade, or *dharmayudha*, is not an uncommon usage in different religions as kings launched their campaign for the expansion of their territories in the name of their religions, time and again, and Islam is no exception. It is believed that Allah wants to spread Islam by the sword. Dr Asghar Ali Engineer, one of the liberal interpreters of Islam, states,

> It is Jihad, which is one of the pillars of Islam precisely because it does not necessarily mean war. Jihad...means utmost effort, not violence and it is obligatory on Muslims to make utmost efforts (in wisely manner) to spread the message of Allah so as to create a just and compassionate society. This is what is obligatory, not waging a war at all. Prophet himself has exemplified it on many occasions especially at the time of Slh-I-Hudabiya (i.e. peace of Hudaibiyah and Fath-I-Mecca). (Engineer 1998)

As for these radical Islamist groups, *jihad* is being used as a cynical ruse to whip up religious fervor for their cause.

> Historically, jihad was used rhetorically by the imperialist powers to justify their worldly expansionist designs. In its original sense, *jihad* was more of an inner moral cleansing for the community. This was called jihad-e-Akbar (The Great Jihad). But now, the whole notion of jihad is being used as an instrument for legitimizing militaristic, monarchic and dictatorial regimes. As for these radical Islamist groups, jihad is being used as a cynical ruse to whip up religious fervor for their cause. (Hasan 2002, 125)

Arundhati Roy points out:

> In 1979 after the Soviet invasion of Afghanistan, the CIA and Pakistan ISI (Inter Service Intelligence) launched the largest covert operation in the history of CIA. Their purpose was to harness the energy of Afghan resistance to the Soviets and expand it into a holy war, an Islamic Jihad, which would turn the Muslim Countries within the Soviet zone of influence, against the communist regime and to eventually destabilize it. When it began it was meant to be Soviet Union's Vietnam. It turned out to be much larger than that. Over the years CIA funded and recruited 100,000 radical Mujahidin from 40 Islamic countries as soldiers for American proxy war (*In Afghanistan*). (Roy 2002)

It is true that some fanatical Muslims found on the fringe use certain medieval interpretation and usage as eternally binding and believe that *kafir*s should be slayed (killed). Also, those hostile to Islam use this term to show the intolerance of Islam.

Most ideologies develop their positive and negative terminologies. Christianity, for example, has derogatory terms such as pagan and nonbeliever, and Hinduism has *maleccha, yavan* (both are derogatory words for Muslims), etc. Islam coined negative terms such as *kufr* (disbelief), *nifaq* (hypocrisy), and *rafz* (rejection or deviation). These terms are many times, or rather most of the times, used against different sects in the same religion. They are tool in the hands of a powerful few with vested interests who use them for their material gains and for the increase of social power. Many Muslim rulers used the word *kafir* while fighting against non-Muslim kings; the same ones then struck compromises also with different kings. We are aware that the Muslim kings were in alliance with Hindu kings and also had Hindu subjects in large numbers, whose religious and other needs were considered by them (e.g., Babar's will to Humayun). These worldly affairs most of the times have been given religious veneer for the benefit of the ruling groups, which if interpreted narrowly can attribute tolerance and intolerance to a particular religion.

War on Terror or Hunting for Oil

'War on Terror' is a euphemism for the United States' aim to take political and military control of different areas of the world, either for the acquisition of oil wealth or for military goals. The acts of terror by the groups scattered here and there have no uniform entity that can be subjected to aggression and eliminated. Since they are scattered and are faceless, it is difficult to identify them and restrain them. In the process, the United States and its allies have been picking areas one after the other and bombing them into deserts. The civilian population and the non-combatants are the biggest victims of the same. Operation Iraqi Freedom was launched after the pretext of dealing with 'weapons of mass destruction' (WMD), failed miserably. United Nations (UN) observer recommendations were bypassed and a war was launched, which met massive resistance from the people of Iraq. It was a war against Iraqi people and incidents like the goings on in the Abu Ghraib prison, where the prisoners were stripped naked and asked to make a human pyramid, and butchering on the Iraqi streets was made the norm by the US army. This army by now is desperate and all the attempts by the United States to outsource the war and to rope in the soldiers of poorer nations have not met with any success, as the United States' aim of making sacrificial goats out of the people of poor countries has failed. Even the US army comprises mainly the underprivileged sections of the US population.

The lack of any credible reason for attacking Afghanistan led many observers to comment that

> [T]he war against Afghans was very much in line with the US's historical role in Afghanistan. In 1970s, the US hired seven different parties of fundamentalists called Mujahidin. These were extremists hired by the CIA during the cold war "to draw the Soviets in to Afghan trap" as later revealed by former National Security Advisor, Zbignew Brezinsky. The CIA gave arms and ammunition to mujahidin…Using these weapons and sophisticated training in the art of terror, these men successfully drove out the

Soviets, but also waged terrible war on their own people killing at least 45000 people in Kabul alone. (Koshy 2002, 62–63)

As the invasion of Afghanistan began just within a few weeks, the United States' claim that they did preparation for this in three weeks is to be taken with a pinch of salt. "Credible reports have appeared that the United States was planning to take military action against Afghanistan to oust Taliban months before September 11" (Koshy 2002, 63). To train Al Qaeda, the United States had spent over 80,000 million dollars and also provided 7,000 tons of armaments, including the stringer missiles. It is for this Kissinger doctrine of 'Asians should be made to fight Asians' that the Muslims youth were indoctrinated in the madrassas with the belief that the communists who had invaded their Afghanistan do not believe in Allah, so they are *kafirs*, and waging a war against them would be *jihad*, and those getting killed in the jihad would go to *jannat*, where all the pleasures, including 72 virgins, will be available for them. Most of the current myths about *jihad*, *kafir*, and terrorists being bred in madrassas start from this massive operation launched by the United States. It is this effort which took the shape of Al Qaeda.

The US propaganda machine keeps dishing out different slogans to serve its foreign policy. In the Cold War era, it was defense of freedom; now it is war on terror. The US media and other media world over following the trails of the United States toe the same line.

The International Tribunal on War Crimes against Afghanistan and Iraq held the United States and its President George W. Bush responsible for the crimes which took place in the region. It held that the United States has been guilty of aggression and consequent crimes (http://www.mindfully.org/Reform/2004/Afghanistan-Criminal-Tribunal10mar04.htm [last accessed on October 10, 2014]).

The Jury of Conscience, in its report released in Istanbul on June 27, 2005, opined that

> [T]his war (on Iraq) as one of the most unjust in history: The Bush and Blair administrations blatantly ignored the massive opposition to the war expressed by millions of people around the world. They embarked upon one of the most unjust, immoral, and cowardly wars in history. The Anglo-American occupation of Iraq of the last 27 months has led to the destruction and devastation of the Iraqi state and society. Law and order have broken down completely, resulting in a pervasive lack of human security; the physical

infrastructure is in shambles; the health care delivery system is a mess; the education system has ceased to function; there is massive environmental and ecological devastation; and, the cultural and archeological heritage of the Iraqi people has been desecrated. (http://www.countercurrents.org/puniyani030109.htm [last accessed on October 10, 2014])

Demonization of Islam: Muslims

Post 9/11, the US media set the scene by coining the term 'Islamic terrorism' and associated Islam with terrorism and fundamentalism in popular perception. Fundamentalism is a broader phenomenon using the identity of many religions. It is necessary to define the term 'fundamentalism' first. It is used in two senses. The orthodox believers of religions or ideologies use it in the sense of going back to the fundamentals of a particular religion or the doctrine. Here, the emphasis is on the original scripture of that particular ideology or religion. The second meaning pertains to the use of religion for political goals of the dominant section of society. In this sense, the selectively culled-out parts of the scriptures or practices, which are against the human rights and equality of weaker sections, are implemented to suppress the libertarian aspirations of these sections. We are using the term in its second sense (political misuse of religion).

> Islamism began in 1920s. The 1980s saw a third generation come of age. Because of their militancy they are mostly referred to as Jehadists, and they state in all clarity that for them jihad is not a matter of moral rearmament (as many Muslims wish jihad to be understood), but armed struggle, their favorite form of self-purification being 'martyrdom'. (Durran 2000)

The concept of *jihad* as armed struggle began from 1927 with a book on *jihad, Al-jihad fil-Islam*; parts of this were translated into English— Muslim self-statements in India and Pakistan (Grunebaum 1970). Just to reiterate, as per the Quran, *jihad* means striving, and expending power and effort to spread the word of Allah to create a just and compassionate society.

The other definition of Islamism is spelt in *Political Islam in the Indian Subcontinent* (Grare 2001). This one goes on to state,

> Islamism can, indeed, not be reduced to religious fervor or to extreme moral rigor-ism characteristic of the Taliban or be reduced to the recourse

to violence. It is defined essentially, in its relationship to politics and hence to the state, by its efforts towards realization of a truly Muslim society.

In Islamism, the conquest of political power is justified by the will to impose the sharia, the sole juridical basis of social relationships before which no other non-Islamic law can exist. "It is an assumption which makes Islamism totalitarian" (Grare 2001). And that conforms to any political system deriving its legitimacy from religion or race. Asghar Ali Engineer, a noted Islamic scholar who has interpreted Islam in a liberal manner, points out,

> The concept of Jihad in Islam has been grossly misunderstood by Muslims and non-Muslims. It is thought that Islam encourages violence and force and that Allah wants to spread Islam with sword or at the point of gun. The acts of some Muslim extremists and terrorists provide proof for this violent image of Islam.... Truth is quite otherwise. (Engineer 1998)

Engineer further points out,

> [T]here is no question of force or violence in spreading Islam. This was popularized by the West after the crusades, which again had nothing to do with spread of religion. It was, in fact the wars of territorial conquest. As far as the spread of religion is concerned Quran rules out violence completely through number of pronouncements. It very forcefully states, *la ikrahfi'al-din* (there is no compulsion in religion) (2:256). Also it makes it plain that one can invite to the path of Allah through wisdom and godly manner (16:125). It is no less important that Quran accepted the truth brought by Prophets before Muhammad. (ibid.)

The Khalistani movement was also fundamentalist in nature. It remained only a movement of rebellion and did not achieve power to exercise its control on the weaker sections. Hindutva had come up in response to the rising secular movement of the Indian National Congress. It did not grow to threaten democracy in India. But during the last two decades, it has assumed menacing proportions due to the rise in the number of middle classes (rich peasants, rich professionals, petty industrialists, etc.). It also derives its legitimacy from a particular version of Hinduism (Brahmanical) and is repressive to women and dalits. The Islamic terrorists harbor the same values, that is, being repressive toward the weaker section.

This use of religion for retrograde politics, which is against the human rights of weaker sections of society, cuts across different religions. It is true that currently the major fundamentalist stream derives its legitimacy from Islam, but that is more because of peculiar circumstances and the role of imperialism and not because of any peculiarity of Islam as a religion.

Hindutva Terrorism

While currently the total focus of investigating agencies in India is to identify acts of terror with Muslim groups and Muslim youth, a very serious omission is taking place. This is due to the conceptual inadequacy of the state machinery or due to motives which are beyond the comprehension of large sections of communities and the activists engaged in issues related to violation of rights of minorities.

Many blasts took place just before some election, some in the aftermath of communal clashes and some at the time of the Friday afternoon prayers. The pattern was so diverse that a single description of these blasts is out of question. Still, there were some common factors in the aftermath of the tragic events. First of all, the police machinery most of the times came up with the theory that the Pakistan-based terrorist groups or local Muslim groups were involved in the blasts; Harkat-ul-Ansar, Lashkar-e-Taiba, Noor-ul-Hooda, Harkat-ul-Jihad, Hizb-ul-Mujahideen, and Indian Mujahideen were blamed most of the times. The claim that the Students Islamic Movement of India (SIMI) is involved as a mastermind, or as an associate, was generally put forward on most occasions.

The usual police claims have been that the culprits were caught with the laptops, identity cards, and other information, which led the police to come to these conclusions. For a large section of the media, these were either poor Muslims trapped in the terror net for the longing for *jannat*, or technology-savvy young men, to create mayhem in India. While no investigation, barring the Malegaon case, proceeded in any meaningful direction, most of the times Muslims, mostly youth, were arrested, tortured, and released after weeks and months due to the lack of any credible evidence.

By now, many cases of blasts starting from the one in Nanded to later ones in Parbhani, Jalgaon, Jalna, Mecca Masjid, Malegaon, Ajmer, and Samjhauta Express have been investigated, and the observations and evidence point toward a pattern of involvement that is emerging, where Bajrang Dal activists are not only carrying guns and swords in a public display of arms but are also actively undertaking acts of terror. It is likely that in many cases their role has remained uninvestigated. There is a deliberate cover-up of these incidents. Some of these leads are not being pursued, while the police are hyperactive in cases where suspected Muslim youth seem to be involved, and that too just on the basis of their confessions. This is a biased attitude of the authorities involved.

A tribunal was organized by Anhad and associated human rights organizations in Hyderabad in 2007 (http://www.anhadin.net/article37. html [last accessed on October 10, 2014]). It had a very demanding task of hearing and verifying the truth of the statements of the various alleged culprits. What was surprising was the gross violation of laws which the police indulged in freely. Not only were the alleged culprits kept in custody and all their rights denied, but their relatives were also not informed; their date of arrest was shown to be much later than the actual date when they were picked up. The torture which they were subjected to is beyond description; the wrecking of poor families as a result of the whole process is shattering. The careers of many promising young men were totally ruined due to such arrests without any proof whatsoever. Is all this reflective of the substandard norms and poor professional training of the officers? Is it rank inefficiency couched in this cruelty are or the tormentors acting like this due to the prevalent biases which have gone deep into the whole society including those of these officers?

The pattern observed in most of the cases was that there were illegal detentions. Following the torture, if a person is to be released, it seems to be a norm that the police takes his/her signature on a blank paper and also threats him/her with dire consequences if he/she goes to human rights activists or lawyers. At times, they are made to shout 'Jai Shri Ram' just to humiliate them. Sometimes, even the possession of Urdu literature is taken as a proof of terrorist links. Third-degree torture of the accused and severe torture to the relatives of the accused to elicit confessions are employed very widely. The accused and their relatives are taken to the police station or other places of detention on false pretexts, and the elementary needs of water and food are not looked at. For permitting the families to see the accused under custody, a bribe is extracted most of the times.

What happens to the future of those who are accused and released later? The students lose their careertrack; at times, colleges do not take them back until court ruling is brought to that effect. The families of the accused get ostracized from the community out of fear. Others stop associating with them. Business of the accused suffers gets a severe setback and at these times banks refuse to give them loans. Some of the accused are also tempted to accept the blames put on them with the carrot dangled in front of them that they will be released. Most of the times, the powers vested with the police seem to be present only through their misuse.

A two-way impression operates in the society: The larger sections of society feel that Muslim terrorists are a big threat to the nation, and Muslims feel that the State is totally partisan and deliberate injustice is being done to them since they are Muslims. Two sets of mechanisms of investigation norms are coming to be rooted. First, Muslim youth are picked up after every blast and are subjected to torture till courts pronounce them not guilty. Second, the Hindus accused in the blasts are treated with kid gloves.

The first major crack in this pattern occurred when in the aftermath of the Malegaon blast, Maharashtra Antiterrorism Squad (ATS) Chief Hemant Karkare meticulously showed the connection of Sadhvi Pragya Singh Thakur and many others from the Hindutva with one or the other offshoot of the Rashtriya Swayamsevak Sangh (RSS) or inspired by the RSS ideology of the Hindu nation, trained in the communal ideology of looking at people through the prism of their religion, and religion alone (http://www.dnaindia.com/india/report_hemant-karkare-feared-for-his-safety-from-hindu-extremists-digvijay-singh_1479752 [last accessed on October 10, 2014]). Karkare's efforts brought out enough skeletons from the cupboard of the Hindutva stable, and somewhere the stubborn police and the political authorities also started looking the other way leading to the plethora of organizations broadly known as the Sangh Parivar (SP). It is also a matter of great concern that the same Hemant Karkare started being abused by Hindutva elements; intimidation and threats to his life began. Incidentally, Karkare was killed on the fateful night of the 26/11 Mumbai terror attack.

Karkare's efforts did initiate a process of bringing the terror investigation on proper track. There were many top RSS functionaries such as Indresh Kumar, and many associates, the major one being Swami Aseemanand of Vishwa Hindu Parishad (VHP), and Vanvasi Kalyan Ashram who started being investigated. Swami Aseemanand was known for his work in *adivasi* (tribal) areas in Dangs, where he whipped up the anti-Christian hysteria leading to anti-Christian violence in the district. He went on to organize a Shabri Kumbh in the area. For this Kumbh, intimidation of *adivasis* was in the air; they were terrorized to attend the Kumbh and some were subjected to *gharvapasi* (return home, conversion to Hinduism). The highlight of the Kumbh was that the top RSS and associated leadership attended it along with the Swami. The Kumbh was the part of anti-minority agenda of the Sangh.

Swami Aseemanand was in the news again for having confessed to the metropolitan magistrate on December 18, 2010, about his and his colleague's involvement in acts of terror (http://www.thehindu.com/news/national/article1073223.ece [last accessed on October 10, 2014]). According to him, while the *jihad* attack on the Akshardham temple in 2002 gave rise to feelings of revenge, this got crystallized after the terrorist attack on the Sankatmochan temple in Varanasi in 2006. After this tragic incident, Swami contacted the others from associated organizations and in a well-planned move organized the terror attacks. He stated:

> We held a meeting at the Valsad residence of Bharat Bhai (Bharat Riteshwar) in June 2006. We planned to carry out blasts at places of worship for Muslims. Sandeep Dange, Bharat Bhai, Sadhvi Pragya, Sunil Joshi, Lokesh Sharma (arrested for Ajmer dargah blast), Ramji Kalsangra and one Amit attended the meeting. We decided to bomb Malegaon, Ajmer dargah, Mecca Masjid and the Samjhauta Express train. Joshi took the responsibility of doing a reconnaissance of all these places. (*Times of India*, January 13, 2011)

Now a detailed police investigation showed the involvement of Hindutva combine: Sadhvi Pragya Singh Thakur (ex-ABVP [Akhil Bhartiya Vidyarthi Parishad] activist), Lt. Col. Prasad Shrikant Purohit, Rt. Major Upadhyay (was chief of Bharatiya Janata Party's [BJP] ex-serviceman cell in Mumbai), Swami Dayanand Pandey (RSS connection, mentor of Abhinav Bharat), Indresh Kumar (member of RSS national executive committee), Sunil Joshi (RSS *pracharak* [full-time propagandist]—later killed), Devender Gupta (RSS pracharak with Abhinav Bharat), Ram Chandra Kalsangra, Sandeep Pandey, and many others.

The confessions of Swami have made many points very clear. The first is that right from the Nanded blast which took place in the house of RSS worker Rajkondawar in 2006, in which two Bajrang Dal workers died, the social activist raised the issue of the involvement of Hindutva elements. On the Nanded issue, a Citizens. Committee also investigated the blast and raised serious issues related to the direction of investigation.

Later, in most of the blasts in Pabhani, Beed, Jalna, and other places in Maharashtra, the same pattern was observed. Social activists kept drawing the attention of the government and media, but their voices remained unheard for a long time. In addition to the attitude of the police, the political leadership, even in non-BJP states and at the Center, refused to take cognizance of the pattern of the blasts and the glaring fallacies in the line of investigation. A large section of media kept quiet and underplayed the involvement of Hindutva elements. While most of the incidents did bag the front-page banner headlines about the involvement of Muslims, and the so-called *jihadi* groups, the voices of victims challenging the police version, and the findings of social activists, were hardly any news, tucked in the back pages, presented in a subdued manner, if at all. During the whole process, a large section of Muslim youth were tortured and many of them had to give up their education and professional careers due to the line of investigation and the treatment from the state which was meted out to them.

Terrorism is a phenomenon which has come up in the guise of religion. It has nothing to do with religion. At the global level, it is the US lust for oil that laid the foundation for Al Qaeda, Taliban, and their horrific acts of terror. In India, the Hindutva groups have resorted to terror on the pretext of avenging the acts of terror carried out by Muslim groups and also to lay the foundation of a Hindu Rashtra. Both these are creating havoc in the life of the society and killing the innocents.

PART I

Terrorism Today: The Global Scene

1

A World Gripped by Terror

On September 11, 2001, two passenger planes crashed into the two towers of the WTC in New York. The third one slammed into the Pentagon in Washington, D.C., and the fourth one, which was probably targeted at either Capitol Hill or the White House, crashed in rural Pennsylvania. Nearly 3,000 people died in this crash who belonged to all countries and religions of the world. There are reports that probably there was one exception to this and that was the Jews who escaped the tragedy due to prior information. Needless to say, most of those who died were innocents.

The targets of the strike were symbols of US might, its ideology, and its policies. It was a shock to the whole world. There were many significant observations on this. To begin with, it was for the first time after the WW II that the United States was attacked on its own soil. It was not done by any 'state' but by a terrorist group. A 'new' weapon was used, a passenger plane of the country which was to be attacked. The scale of the destruction was so massive that some people coined a new term, 'hyper-terrorism', for this event. The aftermath of the destruction was one of total shock and disbelief to begin with. Contrary to usual practice, no terrorist came forward to take responsibility for the attack. The prime suspect of the attack, Osama bin Laden, thanked Allah for this destruction in the United States and called for more attacks on the United States, while disowning the act.

The US administration said that since Osama's statement may contain a hidden coded message for attack on other sites in the United States, it was not shown on the US cables. But the reason was obvious: Osama was linking the attacks to the US army presence in the Middle East and may even have created popular opinion against US interventions in other parts of the world, the major one being the land of Muhammad, West Asia. Undoubtedly, there is very deep resentment in the Middle East against the policies of the United States, but surely they will not endorse the tactics adopted by Osama. It is worth recalling that most of the Muslim countries unequivocally condemned the attack on the WTC. Osama took this opportunity to call for more recruits and asked more Muslim youth to join the *jihad* against America.

George W. Bush, the US President, declared a war on terror, "This will be a monumental struggle between good versus evil.... This crusade, and this war on terrorism is going to take a while" (G.W. Bush, September 12 and 16, 2001, quoted in *Addicted to War; see* Andreas 2004, p 31). The 9/11 attack was presented as a war on America. Interestingly this 'war', unlike the earlier wars in history, was not waged by any other country but a group of individuals. The United States outlined its policy on September 20, 2001, through a speech by the President. This was the speech delivered to the joint session of the US Congress. He said that this act had been carried out by Al Qaeda, which was based in Afghanistan, and had great influence on the Taliban, the then rulers of the country. He demanded that Afghanistan hand over all the Al Qaeda terrorists based in Afghanistan, especially Osama bin Laden. He also made it clear that the demands were not negotiable. In response, Taliban's reply was that the United States should hand over the evidence of Al Qaeda's complicity in the act to a third country. In turn,the United States responded by saying that Osama should be handed over or the country would be attacked. While addressing all the nations of the world, he also went on to declare that "either you are with us or you are against us." Tony Blair, the then Prime Minister of Great Britain, took up the advocacy of US policies right away. The term 'axis of evil' was coined for the countries suspected of harboring the terrorists and their names were put on the hit list of America over a period of time.

Failure of Intelligence!

In the wake of this horrific attack, the US intelligence agencies were severely criticized for their failure. The Federal Bureau of Investigation (FBI) and the CIA were at the receiving end of the criticism. The official line pursued was that it was an intelligence failure. There are doubts whether it was a deliberate failure or a genuine inability to comprehend the nature of danger. The US administration had been getting vague information about the impending attacks by Osama bin Laden; even the possibility of a passenger plane ramming into some building was hinted at by the US allies as early as 1995. This was the first time after the Pearl Harbor attack that the United States was being attacked on its own soil. There are different theories even about this.

One is that the US agencies were working on the assumption that the possibility of attack on US soil did not exist.

> There were many reports that time that Israeli Intelligence had specific information about plans of terrorist attacks inside the US and that this information had been conveyed to the US intelligence agencies. However the Israeli foreign minister Shimon Peres, in an interview to CNN, said Israel had only general information about possible attacks on the US and there was no specific information about targets or modes of attack. (Koshy 2002, 16)

There is extensive documentation on different websites and several books which claim that the US administration had information about the impending attacks, but for some reason, which is becoming clearer by the day, it chose not to take preemptive actions. The nature of these urgent warnings converged in a manner specifying that the attacks would occur between early and mid-September as a likely watch date. Sebastian (2002, 21) points out that the *Sunday Telegraph* (London) did report that the Israeli intelligence service Mossad had delivered a warning to the FBI and CIA in August that many followers of Osama were slipping into the country to prepare a major assault on the United States. According to Russian press reports, the Russian Intelligence notified the CIA during the summer that 25 terrorist pilots had been getting training specifically for suicide missions. "In an interview on September 15 with MSNBC, Russian President Vladimir Putin confirmed that he had ordered Russian Intelligence in August to warn the US Government 'in the strongest possible terms' of imminent attacks on airports and government buildings..." (Ruppert 2002). Yet, despite this extensive forewarning of attacks, the Bush administration failed to act (Ahmed 2002).

There were unconfirmed reports that the US President had been briefed by the CIA about the imminent attack by the passenger plane within the United States, and that no cognizance of this was taken by the administration. One Minneapolis FBI agent reported about Moussaoui, a French Moroccan immigrant who wanted to learn how to fly the aeroplane, and was not interested in the takeoff and landing part of flying a Boeing 747. "One e-mail from a Minneapolis FBI agent described Moussaoui as someone who might fly a jumbo jet into WTC. Both reports were ignored by FBI headquarters" (Koshy 2002, 19).

All these prior warnings and intelligence reports were not taken seriously, and many senators and others were upset by this. Was this deliberate or a slip on the part of most 'efficient' intelligence agency in the world?

State Response on the Doomsday

The tragedy of such a high order brought into focus the events of the day. While the relief and rehabilitation work being was undertaken on a massive scale, the alertness of the state was very visible. But what was happening when the hijacked planes were flying in the airspace for close to an hour, and when did the concerned authorities come to know about the hijacking?

There are various standing operating procedures for intercepting errant airplanes flying in the US skies. A fleet of fighter planes is always at hand to intercept such aircrafts and can be activated within minutes. What happened on that fateful day? Dick Cheney, the Vice President, stated that the fighter planes were not available that day. This is difficult to believe as it goes against the basic standing operating procedures. It is surprising that despite four planes being hijacked and for a lot of time in the airspace, the US security system failed to act. "For 50 minutes on September 11, in direct contravention of established policy, no fighters were scrambled to intercept two outstanding hijacked airliners even though it was known attacks were in progress" (Ruppert 2002).

Thomas Sebastian writes,

> U.S. air safety and air defense emergency systems are activated in response to problem every day. On 9-11 they failed despite, not because of, the

extreme nature of the emergency. This could only happen if individuals in high positions worked in a coordinated way to make it fail. (2002, 38)

What was the President of the United States doing on that day? To begin with, he was not informed for 35 minutes that the planes had been hijacked. When he was informed, he did not display any shock and continued to speak in the classroom where he was addressing school children. It seems that the President already knew about the WTC event, even as his motorcade was speeding toward the school.

Peter, as you know, the President's down in Florida talking about education. He got out of his hotel suite this morning, was about to leave, reporters saw the White House Chief of Staff Andy Card, whisper into his ear. The reporter said to the President, "do you know what's going on in New York?" He said he did, and he said he will have something about it later. His first event is half an hour at an elementary school in Sarasota, Florida. (ABC News Special Report, September 11, 2001)

According to Mary Schiavo, former Inspector for the US Department of Transportation (1900–1996), 682 hijackings have occurred worldwide since 1972. All were thoroughly investigated. But these four hijackings were not investigated. Why? The administration blocked any move to probe this attack. The Enron case was investigated by eight committees, while a single one, largely behind closed doors, undertook the half-hearted reporting of this attack.

A few Pentagon officials canceled their travel plans on September 11 on the grounds of security concerns. What does this suggest? Also, the United States has not been able to put forward any credible report evidence of its version of the events that took place on September 11. The only thing they have done is to "successfully put forward their version of the events through media blitzkrieg, as a prelude to attack Afghanistan."

These observations lead to very uncomfortable conclusions. Was the US administration taken by surprise by these events or was there prior knowledge? Why was the threat not dealt with effectively as there was a possibility of the same? Some analysts conclude that

[T]he events of September 11 were planned years in advance, with the groundwork being carefully laid by propaganda campaign orchestrated to convince public that United States has plausible sophisticated nemesis with the motive, means and opportunity, to perpetuate the devastating act of terror against Americans. Towards that Saudi Arabia and Pakistan have been used as the primary proxy agents, setting up and financing the infrastructure of Al Qaeda in Afghanistan. Through Madrassa based in Pakistan, Saudi and Yemenite militants were instructed in the Saudi brand of Wahabi Islam and subsequently 'graduated' to camps that were set up in Afghanistan-again, under Saudi and Pakistani sponsorship. In the US, the operative agents were based mostly in New York City and Florida. (Kupferberg 2002)

The Day After

The reactions to this grave act were very diverse. Osama thanked Allah for this happening because according to him, the United States is the enemy of the Muslim world, and is responsible for grave tragedies in West Asia. The view prevalent in certain sections that the United States has been punished for its crimes is very unethical, as the victims of the tragedy have been the innocents, those who had nothing to do with the US policies which have brought misery to the Muslim world. George Bush resorted to anti-Muslim rhetoric that the attacks were master-minded by those who are opposed to freedom and democracy. Broadly, Samuel Huntington's thesis of 'Clash of Civilizations' that the advanced Western civilization is faced with a threat from the backward Islamic civilization came to the fore.

While Osama used the label of *jihad* for his acts, Bush retaliated by declaring a crusade; it was christened 'War on Terror', and the war was titled as 'Operation Enduring Freedom'. The ideological raison d'etre was quickly constructed against the terrorists, "We know exactly who these people are and which governments are supporting them." This is contrary to the focus of the terrorist attack. If they were against the values of liberty, they could have targeted the Statue of Liberty, but clearly they attacked the sites that are associated with US might, military, and economy. This war began with bombing Afghanistan; it was precision bombing flattening the cities of Afghanistan. Cluster bombs were dropped in large areas. Food packets were dropped along with the bombs with an idea that people dying of bomb attacks "knew the generosity of the United States and its allies." as they would not be hungry before they embraced death. The civilian population was driven away from homes for the fear of bombs and later had to face the bullets when in the open. The US administration refused to consider any alternative to war. The Taliban government, in a conciliatory gesture, asked for evidence against bin Laden; the US response was a threat to hand over Osama or be prepared to face the war.

This was the time when millions were already facing shortages of supplies and basic amenities. The US aggression worsened the situation and innocent civilians suffered tremendously. The number of killings in Afghanistan went into thousands. But the target of the attack, Osama, was as safe as George Bush himself. The irony of this war was that the planes of the richest and most powerful country in the world were attacking the civilians of one amongst the poorest of poor nations. There was intense anger amongst a section of Muslim countries. There were angry demonstrations in many Muslim countries. Unfazed by all this, the United States thundered to warn other nations into bowing to its wishes, "Every nation in the region has a decision to make. Either you are with us or you are with the terrorists. From this day forward, any nation that continues to harbor or support terrorism will be regarded as a hostile regime" (Murlidharan 2001).

The lack of any credible reason for attacking Afghanistan led many observers to comment that

> [T]he war against Afghans was very much in line with the US's historical role in Afghanistan. In 1970s, the US hired seven different parties of fundamentalists called Mujahidin. These were extremists hired by the CIA during the cold war "to draw the Soviets in to Afghan trap" as later revealed by former National Security Advisor, Zbignew Brezinsky. The CIA gave arms and ammunition to mujahidin.... Using these weapons and sophisticated training in the art of terror, these men successfully drove out the Soviets, but also waged terrible war on their own people killing at least 45000 people in Kabul alone. (Koshy 2002, 62–63)

As the invasion of Afghanistan began within just a few weeks, the US claim that they prepared for this in three weeks is to be taken with a pinch of salt. "Credible reports have appeared that the US was planning to take military action against Afghanistan to oust Taliban months before September 11" (Koshy 2002, 63).

Iraq as the Next Target

The world had hardly recovered from the impact of the Afghan war that the air became heavy with the anticipated war against Iraq. Various phenomenon were in the air: WMD, biological weapons, and Saddam Hussain's atrocities against the Iraqi people. What was the projected was that the US armies would be sort of liberation armies, going to provide relief to the oppressed Iraqis.

Iraq had witnessed an earlier attack from the armies of the United States and its allies. In 1993, the United States had launched war against Iraq for 'freedom and justice'. The real reasons for the intervention in West Asia have been oil, but different slogans have been cooked up in defense of the efforts to control the oil reserves and the military control in this area. The US State Department had once declared that oil is "a stupendous source of strategic prizes of world history." As is well known, nearly 65 percent of the world's known oil resources lie in this region. Henry Kissinger, the US Secretary in the Nixon era, was forthright to declare that, "Oil is much too important a commodity to be left in the hands of the Arabs" (quoted in *Addicted to War*; see Andreas 2004, 29). The US Government had been planning to control this region through wars and occupations since 1979 when Jimmy Carter, the then US President, declared that "any threat to Persian gulf oil will be repelled by any means necessary, including military force."

In Iraq, the added reason was that Iraq had been given arms by the United States itself to wage a war against Iran post Ayatollah Khoemini revolution. This change of guards in Iran had heavy anti-US overtones and the United States was labeled as the 'Great Satan'. Iran was seen as the major threat to US interests in the oil region. Also, the United States whole heartedly supported Iraq's war against Iran and supplied it with all possible weapons, biological (anthrax) and chemical (poison gas). The Pentagon also supplied intelligence to Iraq which was crucial in its planning of the war. At this time, Kuwait was an ally of Iraq and the United States went to the extent of sending a naval armada to the Persian Gulf to save its oil tankers. The United States went on to destroy the oil platform of Iran during that period.

After the war, the United States realized that Iraq was now equipped with weapons and could be a counter to its own hegemony. Iraq was in a way lured to attack Kuwait. The Iraqi invasion was a response to the economic pressure on it by the United States, Saudi Arabia, and Kuwait. Kuwait had been ruled by Iraq for the past 2,000 years. Most of the Iraqi governments since the 1922 mandate had been laying territorial claim on Kuwait. Kuwait was very provocative in its oil dispute with Iraq. Saddam Hussein's party, Ba'ath, came up with a plan to restore Iraqi sovereignty on Kuwait. Saddam wanted to sound the idea out with the United States before venturing on invasion. "To this day Iraqi officials insist that Saddam's fatal meeting with US ambassador April Glaspie was an event of decisive importance. Glaspie was sympathetic to their case, was informed of Iraq's plans and gave her de facto approval" (Ali 2003, 143). After the occupation of Kuwait, and the US turnaround, with the intervention of the Soviet foreign minister, a deal for unilateral withdrawal of Iraq was negotiated. The deal was totally rejected by the United States. Iraq, an ally of the United States till then, came to be immediately branded as 'Arab Hitler'. The US attack was massive and resulted in intense destruction of the Iraqi land. With the invasion by the United States, Iraqi soldiers had begun to retreat, but their way was blocked, the gate was closed, and thousands of Iraqi soldiers were massacred along with demolishing the war machine of Iraq, which the United States itself had helped build. Nearly 150,000 Iraqis died during this Gulf War. More died of diseases and starvation. Waterborne diseases took a very heavy toll on the lives of the Iraqis as the United States systematically destroyed Iraq's electrical sewage treatment and water treatment plants. Over half a million children died due to the effects of war. This also put severe economic sanctions on Iraq's economy, crippling it.

"The bombing of Iraq began on January 16, 1991. Far from restricting themselves to evicting Iraq from Kuwait, or attacking only military targets, the US led coalition's bombing campaign systematically destroyed Iraq's civilian infrastructure, including electricity generation, communication, and water and sanitation facilities" (Research Unit for Political Economy 2002, 35).

Oil corporations and royal families of Kuwait, bankers, and builders were to celebrate the whole exercise with huge profits. The US war industry got a big boost due to this war. After this, US armies came to be permanently stationed in Saudi Arabia. The US Secretary of State

Madeleine Albright justified this by saying that it is a price worth paying to protect the sovereignty of the Sheikh of Kuwait.

The sanctions imposed by the UN in the wake of its occupation of Kuwait crippled it very badly. These sanctions continued till the second attack on Iraq. These sanctions emasculated Iraq militarily and weakened it economically, affecting its social life to a great extent. The effect of the sanctions can be gauged from the fact that Denis Halliday, UN Humanitarian Coordinator in Iraq from 1997 to 2008, resigned in protest against the operation of sanctions, which he termed as deliberate 'genocide'. This genocide was a deliberate US policy. On May 12, 1996, Madeleine Albright was asked by Lesley Sthal of CBS Television: "We have heard that half a million children have died. I mean, that's more than died in Hiroshima. And, you know, is the price worth it?" Albright replied: "I think this is a very hard choice, but the price, we think the price is worth it" (Research Unit for Political Economy 2002, 39).

Re-destroying Iraq

The US administration was out to occupy Iraq on the pretext of the 9/11 attack. This was in a sense the 'unfinished' agenda of the Gulf War. The United States did intend to restructure and reorder the world according to its designs. The 'New World Order' design of Bush senior remained incomplete so far as Saddam Hussein was in power in Iraq. The United States now wanted to use the pretext provided by the 9/11 attack to fulfill its agenda. Bush Jr began talking about Saddam being an evil man and the need for the regime change in Iraq.

The first step in this direction was to link Al Qaeda with Iraq. There was no connection; none could be proved barring CIA Director George Tenet's testimony before Congress that there was 'mutual antipathy' that Iraq and Al Qaeda shared against the United States, the hint being that sharing this mutual antipathy, they must be acting hand in glove against the interests of the United States. Obviously, this was too weak a justification for launching a war against Iraq. And then there was the pretext of dealing with weapons of mass destruction (WMD). Barring the fact that this made the word WMD a popular one, there was no evidence whatsoever of the same. The UN Inspector's team failed to find any evidence of WMD in 1998 as well as in 2003. One of the letters published in *Weekly Standard* and signed by 37 well-known policy experts and columnists underlined the US plans in the clearest terms:

> It may be that the Iraqi government provided assistance in some form to the recent attack on United States. But even if evidence does not link Iraq directly to the attack, any strategy aiming at the eradication of terrorism and its sponsors must include determined efforts to remove Saddam Hussein from power in Iraq. Failure to undertake such a will constitutes an early and perhaps decisive surrender in the war on International terrorism. (Koshy 2002, 120)

The situation can be summed up as the US was wanting to attack and was looking for a pretext.

> The existence of the document that outlined significant aspects of a 'concept' for a war against Iraq… indicates an advanced stage of planning in the military. The concept for such a plan is highly evolved and is apparently working its way through military channels. Once a consensus is reached on the concept, the steps towards assembling a final war plan and, most importantly, the element of timing for ground deployment and commencement of an air was representing the final sequencing that Mr. Bush will have to decide. (Schmitt 2002)

By this time, the UN and its Security Council had been totally bypassed and the earlier facade of UN approval was done away with. In a way, before invading Iraq, the United States and the UK proceeded to prepare the coffin of the world body, UN, which had played a significant role in containing wars in the decades gone by. During this war, the myth of Darul Islam (the Muslim community of the world) was also shattered. The United States had won over major Islamic and other countries to its side. The only opposition which remained was the Global Peace movement, scattered yet very visible, when millions marched against the US invasion of Iraq, in New York, London, and various cities all over the world.

The noose around Iraq was being tightened by the day. Despite the report of weapon's inspector, the United States preceded its invasion of Iraq. The US aggressiveness was unnerving. The Iraqi army did not have sophisticated weaponry to halt this aggression. The sanctions of previous years had crippled the Iraqi defense. It was quite a walkover for the US army, barring at a few places. The resistance grew later and took a heavy toll on the invading army. The naked face of perversion became obvious in the Abu Ghraib prison, photographs from which came to light. The Iraqi prisoners were stripped naked and were subjected to all sorts of humiliations. One instance was where they were asked to make human pyramids, and the second picture, which speaks thousand words, was the one in which one young US army recruit, a girl, put a dog strap around the neck of a naked prisoner. The reaction to this was of shock, but the US administration soon wriggled out of it on one or the other pretext. Unlike in 1991, the protest against the US war started surfacing in the Arab world and also all over the world.

The US designs in Iraq were to unfold gradually after its occupation of Afghanistan. The United States started saying that Iraq is in possession of WMD. UN commissioners were deputed in Iraq who unequivocally gave the report that Iraq is not in possession of any such weapons. Undeterred by that, the United States went on to attack and occupy Iraq, marching millions of its soldiers. It was said that this army was the liberation army and would be welcomed with roses by the victims of Saddam. Soon, imaginary roses turned into real guns and the resistance movement picked up in Iraq. So far, while the US army has 'liberated', by killing over 500,000 Iraqis, the resistance reaction has sent over 5,000 body bags to the United States, containing the bodies of US soldiers on the 'mission democracy', the pet slogan of the United States in its design to control the world and appropriate the oil resources in the region.

There is another analogy which comes to one's mind. When the British ruled India, they also partitioned the country. US policies have already aggravated sectarian divides between Shias, Sunnis, and Kurds. The imminent aggravation of civic strife is on the cards. Who does one blame it on?

As an aside, in the Indian scenario, the RSS has been the permanent defender of the US attacks and aggressions around the world. Starting from the US butchery in Vietnam to the current US polices in Iraq, this organization has been supporting all of these as a most loyal retainer of

Uncle Sam. At the time of the attack on Iraq by the US armies, the RSS chief vociferously defended the US aggression.

India

Islam and Muslims as the culprit was part of the ideology of the Hindutva movement of the Hindu Mahasabha and the RSS at the time of the freedom struggle. The decline of sections of the Muslim and Hindu elite (landlords and kings) threw up communal organizations at the time of the freedom struggle. The mass movement for freedom struggle was going on under the leadership of Mahatma Gandhi, in which the Indian National Congress was the main organization, and this movement drew from the values of Mohandas Karamchand Gandhi, Bhagat Singh, and B.R. Ambedkar. This movement was based on liberty, equality, fraternity, and justice. Most Indians supported this movement, while a miniscule section remained aloof. This section which remained aloof from freedom movement was the one mentioned above.

Since the average Hindus and Muslims did not support their politics, they resorted to spreading hatred toward the people of other communities on the grounds of religion, and this in turn resulted in the worsening of the intercommunity relations and later, in the formation of Pakistan. While Pakistan, under the tutelage of US imperialism, remained a mullah military complex, the intermittent flashes of democratic regimes were short-lived breaths of fresh air. The condition of the Hindu minority suffered a severe blow. Later, Pakistan itself got vivisected into two, Pakistan and Bangladesh, where again the condition of the Hindu minority is nothing to commend. In India, while the government tried to be secular, there were insurmountable obstacles in this path.

The RSS-trained volunteers infiltrated different wings of State since the early 1930s and 1940s, and this picked up in a big way after the Janata Party regime of 1977, when the erstwhile Bharatiya Jansangh became part of this party. Even the party which ruled more often, Congress, had Hindu right-wing leanings right from the beginning and it depended on the quality of leadership to restrain this tendency. After the Nehru era, there were many compromises on the values of secularism. The seeds of

Babri Masjid–Ram temple dispute were sown in 1949, when a group of pro-RSS sadhus installed the idols of Ram Lalla in the masjid (mosque). Nehru urged upon the Uttar Pradesh Chief Minister to have these idols evacuated, but the local district magistrate was an RSS man and he ensured the continuation of the presence of Ram idols in the mosque. As such, the inherent communal propaganda did result in low-grade communal hatred, but it was too minor. After the Jabalpur riots of 1961, it came to the surface, and since then communal violence started taking place on a regular basis. The period of 1980 saw the worsening of this scenario. This was also a period when the dalit assertion started increasing, the women's groups started demanding their rights, and as a clever response to distract the social attention from these core issues, the anti-minority tirades were stepped up (Puniyani 2001). Around this time, VHP brought to the fore the Ram temple issue and it started getting a social response from sections of the society. After the demolition of the masjid, anti-Muslim hysteria went through the roof and one witnessed the horrific Mumbai riots. By now, the Muslims and Islam had started being projected as the villains of peace. Meanwhile, the unresolved India–Pakistan relations started manifesting in the issue of Kashmir. In popular psyche, terrorism in Kashmir and later in different parts of the country got inseparably associated with Islam and Muslims. This anti-Muslim hatred played a major part in the intensification of the Gujarat violence. The intensity of the Gujarat riots was also because of the fact that it was RSS progeny that was at the heart of the riots, and so the acts of commission of Modi in Gujarat further polarized the communities along religious lines. By the end of the Gujarat violence, the association between Islam, Muslims, and terrorism got firmly rooted as a part of social common sense.

Muslims–Islam: Villains of Peace?

While globally Islam became the most visible 'other' of US imperialism and its attempts to control the oil wealth, in many countries, this got further boosted after the 9/11 attack. Today, while a large part of the world is suffering from poverty, hunger, disease, and misery, the major problem being projected is that of terrorism, Muslims, and Islam.

As the ghastly tragedy of 9/11 shocked the world, the US media and other media jumped to accentuate the propaganda against Muslims and Islam. This is what was subtly going on since the 1980s. Now this came to the surface, preceding the attacks by the United States on Afghanistan and Iraq. The thesis propounded by Huntington (1996) became the foremost ideology acting as a cover for the US designs in the world in general and in West Asia in particular.

2

Changing Goals of Colonialism– Imperialism: From 'White Man's Burden' to 'War Against Terror'

Terrorism as it is being witnessed today has a lot to do with the policies of colonial powers of the past and imperialists powers today. Colonialism came to be projected under the banner of 'white man's burden'. In India, colonialism left behind the phenomenon of communalism, politics in the name of religion. These political currents have some relations to terrorist violence. On the other hand, we see that the goals of imperialism have resulted in the rise of the terrorist violence in the name of Islam. In this chapter, we trace the deeper dynamics of both these processes.

Colonialism: Secularization

The events, the phenomena, which were to have deeper repercussions on the societal and political systems all over the world, were to begin with the changes that led to reformation, modern values, industrial revolution, and colonialism. Some of the European states that had undergone industrial transformation also saw the changes in social hierarchies, increase in the industrial production leading them to search for markets and in turn colonize the countries where they began with the search for markets and ended up with plundering the colonies for raw materials and economically exploiting them.

The economic changes resulted in the disintegration of feudalism. The Renaissance came in as bringing fresh values in Europe; it began around AD 1300 with renewed interest in the study of texts of ancient Greece and Rome. It was in fact an ensemble of achievements in philosophy, art, literature, religion, politics, and science, more related to contemporary achievements. Reformation was to herald the disintegration of the feudal system. It began as a revolt against the authority of the Catholic Church and the Pope and led to Protestantism and setting up of Protestant Churches from the early 16th century. During the late 16th century, the Catholic reformation added on to the collapse of feudal systems, laying the foundation for a capitalist economy. Use of money in economic transactions increased. Trade and manufacture laid the foundations of capitalist economy, the one geared for making profit. Now, money and not land became the measure of wealth. This was a major transition from the earlier times.

The authority of the clergy had monopolized knowledge. With the Renaissance, this started breaking. Earlier, philosophers' views had to be sanctioned by the Church for them to be accepted. With the Renaissance thinkers rejecting the notion that the clergy is the sole source of knowledge, the path for development of modern science opened up, and this then laid the foundation for technological advancement and increased production of goods. Discovery of trade routes and newer countries by the European countries opened up the way for trade and future colonization.

Another important phenomenon which needs to be understood is the rise of nation states. Initially, kings had little powers and they had to depend on the feudal lords for support. With the rise of merchants, trading far and wide, they could gather more support and strengthen their organizations. Earlier, the boundaries of estates and kingdoms had no rational basis.

> At a later stage in European history, some individual feudal territories evolved into something much more like modern nation state. Kingdoms emerged with distinct boundaries within which central authorities claimed exclusive jurisdiction, sophisticated judicial systems with rights of appeal from local courts up to center, a taxation system divorced from the rents payable to the owners of land, and in some cases representative legislative assemblies. (Tansey 2000, 32)

This process had the ingredient of the broadening of the language, and later, the process of colonization, "The rise of national languages also helped in the process of emergence of strong nation states by strengthening national consciousness. The process of colonial expansion which started with the discovery of new sea routes and new land was also connected with these developments" (Dev 1999, 192). Nation states put an end to the anarchy of the feudal times.

The changes in the production system from the syndicates of the craftsmen to industries laid the basis of the coming up of new industrialists and also the workers. These changes affected women's lives a great deal. The rise in industrial production faced obstacles from the old power centers of kings and feudal lords. This is what led to these new classes demanding the principles of liberty, equality, and fraternity. The divine right of kings and nobles came to be challenged and laid the basis for struggle, leading to democracies and the new social relations in some European countries. The most significant of such changes, which occurred in a striking fashion, were in France and Europe. These took place in many other European countries in some or the other form. The core of these modern transformations was the changeover to technology-based industrial production, end of the authority of kings and nobles, and the end of the alliance of the king and the clergy, with the clergy's power thereby being relegated to the background.

England's revolution began in the 17th century with a conflict between the king and the parliament over the question of power. The civil war that followed led to the execution of the king and the establishment of a republican form of government. Initially, new gentry controlled the parliament. Many years passed before the concepts of democracy could take root in the society and people at large could become part of the electoral process. Later, the British kept the king as the formal head of the democratically elected government.

Rise of Capitalism

The new system of society that emerged in Europe in the 15th century was capitalism. Productivity increased due to technological innovations.

> The medieval guilds went out of their way to obstruct improvement in the techniques of labor organization, fearing that this might lead to some growing richer than their fellows.... Higher labor productivity and considerable increase in the volume of production in various industries led to division of production process into number of separate operations or processes each carried out by separate guild. (Manfred 1974, 233)

In a capitalist economy, the means of production are under the owner ship of private individuals and production is motivated by the goal of profit. Goods are meant for sale in the market, and hence the profit motive. This leads to the desire to produce more goods that prompts the use of machines in the production process—the Industrial Revolution. In Europe during the Industrial Revolution, this also started changing the social relations. The extreme form of this was manifested in the French revolution where the monarchy was overthrown and the formal principles of liberty, equality, and fraternity came into being as the guiding principles of society.

This era saw two main developments. One was the replacement of kingdoms by democracies in certain States. The basic principle of these two is contradictory. Kingdoms are based on the divine principle, inheritance, the feudal structures, and the hierarchy of class and gender. The democratic principle in theory started emerging as the system based on popular franchise. Popular will formally came up through elections in due course. The second was the process of secularization in which the role of the clergy was marginalized and religion became a personal matter instead of being the affiliate of the State's power structure.

Secularization

From the 17th century onward, discoveries of science began challenging the deeply held beliefs and faith that were the integral part of the broad canvass of religion. This ran parallel to the social changes where the new classes realized that the feudal classes, kings, are parasitical in nature, not contributing to work but consuming maximum and enjoying infinite rights, most of them under the cloak of religion. This phenomenon of opposition to the premodern classes was first observed in Europe, where the medieval period was characterized by the supremacy of the church over all aspects of life. There were quite a few who had, through lifelong dedication, discovered the secrets of nature, but were seen as heretics, blasphemous, or otherwise. For example, in 1553, Servatus was burnt at the stake for publishing his work in the field of medicine, which was labeled by the church as being against the idea of the Trinity. Similarly, Palissy, who was a great natural scientist with several contributions in the field of minerals, geology, and chemistry, had to die in prison in 1590 for converting to Protestantism. Copernicus had to present his discovery that the Earth went around the Sun merely as a mathematical formulation rather than as a real-life phenomenon for the fear of persecution. At the same time, the broad social layers realized that they had different aspirations than those propagated by the clergy and imposed by kingdoms. Their awareness was the root of democratic movements, which assumed the form of revolutions at places.

The European secularization movement took root during the period of Renaissance and French Enlightenment. The vast mass of peasantry crushed under feudal exploitation could see the liberatory potential of the slogan 'Liberty, Equality, and Fraternity', the call given by the rising French bourgeoisie to break the hold of the feudalism–church nexus on the society. The struggle against feudal absolutism also involved struggle against the hold of church/religion on the society. Here, the requirements of the newly emerging industries required the peasants to be released from the social grip of feudal lords and the concomitant religious grip of the church. It is in this backdrop that one can begin to understand the meaning of social norms developing around modern rationality. The peasants and women joined the opposition to the kingdom–clergy nexus as they foresaw their own liberation from the clutches of social and gender hierarchies.

Similar to the French experience, the Industrial Revolution in England projected the ideal of a democratic form of government, and the realization of the rights of individuals as citizens proved to be a turning point. Thus, the secularization of civil society and polity was actually the culmination of numerous factors into new scientific discoveries and technological advancement, which revolutionized the modes of production in both agriculture and industry, unleashing novel socio-religious processes, renaissance, and reformation. Navigation and new markets, the emergence and rise of a new class of the bourgeoisie, and the consequent contractual relationship brought in free labor and capital accumulation. It ran *pari passu* (at an equal rate or pace) with the people's movements for equality in all spheres of life.

Thus, modernity and secularization do not just emerge from ideological constructs of the philosophers and ideologues. Primarily, these twin processes are the outcome of the struggles of the emerging bourgeoisie (industrialists and their paraphernalia), and the expression of the struggles of peasants under the clutches of feudal lords. These processes derive social roots from these sectors of society that emerge pari passu with the development of science and technology, which form the infrastructure of the newer production processes.

Modernity and secularization take place at a particular juncture in history when the newer production processes are trying to integrate the achievements of science and technology into their gambit. The newer production processes require a labor force which till that time is not `free floating', gripped as it is by the traditional hierarchies, at the service of feudal lords, and legitimized by the clergy. The prevalent system is a mix of prescientific social wisdom and gender-related hierarchies which are sustained by the preaching of clergy, priests, *acharyas* (teachers), and mullahs. The secularization movement is heralded by two parallel but opposite groups whose interests are common at this point of time. The rising industrialist needs more social powers, and a labor force, which can be hired on contractual terms. The victims of prevalent hierarchies, the poor peasantry, look forward to the work in industries as a 'relative' liberation from the prevalent oppressive social structures. And along with it goes the struggle for social consent, ideas in social space where the scientific reason battles it out with the prescientific social ideas.

Thus, the complex of modernity/secularization cannot be located in any one single arena; it is a comprehensive arrival of newer social relationships (industrialist–labor: on social contractual terms), newer rationality (around science and reason) on the one hand and the feudalism–church nexus (based on birth-based hierarchies) and prescientific social ideas on the other.

Secularization in India

The secularization process in India has been an extremely complex and painful one. The European powers were out to colonize the rest of the world to enrich their industrial development and create markets for their industrial products. India came mainly under the sway of the British who colonized the country, and keeping their needs in mind, initiated a ruthless plunder of India's wealth and raw materials. They increased the taxation on land, forced the shift to cash crops, and simultaneously ensured intense plunder by laying down railways and telegraph as the efficient means of transport and communication. To supplement their needs for trained–educated manpower, they introduced English education in the country. To support their efforts, many Indians came forward as their 'assistant', who themselves started laying down the foundations of modern industries and eventually graduated as 'modern' business professionals. At this time, these modern ideas also found their way through the newer education system and through a class of intelligentsia who started going to England for their education.

This process again required the release of peasants from their 'ties' to the lands, and subjugation to the feudal lords and Brahmans. Simultaneously, we see the twin movements that contributed to the secularization process. The first of these was the independence movement, aimed against the control of colonial masters, and the second was a series of regional movements against the social hierarchy, caste system, and gender oppression, aimed to gain self-respect and break the social stranglehold of landlords, Brahmans, and the caste system.

This exposure to new learning also laid the foundation of the Indian renaissance. The positive and negative factors of alien rule, for example, Western liberalism, free press, modern system of communications, along with racial arrogance, economic exploitation of India, and assertion of cultural superiority by the English, filled the Indian mind with a new spirit of national consciousness. The British policies put into motion a number of contradictory processes. The development of modernity was not just against the religious clergy and landlords but had to take on the British rulers also.

The spread of colonial powers affected the Islamic world also. By the beginning of the 16th century, almost the entire Arab world came under the domination of the Ottoman Empire.

Egypt, Syria, Tripoli, Tunis and Algiers in the north and Yemen in the Southern end of Arabian peninsula was incorporated into empire, lorded over by the Ottomans. The Turkish rulers were called sultan and the myth of caliphate which survived through the Mamluke period in Egypt finally vanished. The Ulama once again accepted the new reality and found justification for the Ottoman rule. (Engineer 1994, 82)

This hegemony of the Ottomans came to an end during WW I with the help of British power. This also laid the foundation of the new nationalism. The Ottoman Empire was not a monolith. It was "not so much a single community as a group of communities each of which claimed the immediate loyalty of its members. These communities where regional, religious or functional; or, to some extent, a mixture of all these" (Hourani 1962, 29).

The Turkish Sultan used Islam as a cover for his rule. He projected himself as a protector of Islam vis-à-vis Western rulers, also to win over the loyalty of Arabs who, in one way or the other, resented non-Arab domination. Arabs and Islam were intertwined. The two ethnic ruling classes had deeper collaboration in ruling the empire.

With the establishment of the colonial rule, new challenges came up in the society and these were projected as challenges to Islam. Ottoman rulers started adjusting to the new system and political equilibrium.

In the last quarter of 19th century the crisis of Islam became much more acute. It was no longer possible for Arab intellectuals to take a detached attitude towards the west as it became apparent that France's occupation of Algiers was not an isolated incident in a relatively remote regency of Ottoman Empire but a prelude to imposing western hegemony along the whole coast of Mediterranean. (Mansfield 1978, 75)

The colonial period for the Ottoman Empire had a peculiarity. Europe had mainly feudalism, the peasants, and extraction of surplus from peasants by the feudal lords. In the Ottoman Empire, barring Egypt, most of the areas were mainly subsisting on trade, merchants being prominent in society. The colonial rule resulted in the breakup of the Ottoman Empire. The countries to emerge from this empire were Iraq, Syria, Lebanon, and Transjordan. "Strong bourgeoisie class had not emerged from these countries (although the traditional mercantile elements did exist and exerted some pressure) to champion the cause of nationalism as we understand today" (Engineer 1994, 90).The interpretation of the social norms kept changing with the times and the concept of Islamic state underwent drastic changes. These concepts also kept changing from interpreter to interpreter.

Colonialism affected the Muslim countries in a serious way. Russia and England set up banks in Iran to have economic control. Southern Iran came under British hegemony and northern Iran under Russian influence, while central Iran was open to both. Britain also came to take control of Afghanistan. With the Russian revolution in 1917, Russia gave up its control over northern Iran, and Britain came to occupy the same. With the discovery of oil in Iran, the foreign oil companies increased their domination. Meanwhile, Germany increased its hold over Turkey. With the defeat of Germany in WW I, the hold of Germany on Turkey came to an end and the countries under Turkey's control, Syria, Iraq, and Palestine, and Arabia's control were passed on to Britain. In due course, imperialist countries' policies started getting shaped by the lust to control oil resources in the Middle East. American oil companies in partnership with England and France got oil concessions in Arabia. Egypt and Sudan were won over by Britain.

Islamic states were mainly feudal, with trade, agriculture, and craft as major occupations and natural resources as the main assets. There was a great diversity; it changed from country to country and region to region. Colonialism was imposed on these states, like in other states, as an alien rule, which was more interested in extracting raw materials and benefiting in power equations. This interaction of the modern system was very peculiar the world over. On the one hand, it exposed the people of colonies to plunder, exploitation, and injustice of the worst order, and on the other hand, it gave them a glimpse of the values of liberty, equality, and fraternity from a distance. The ruling classes of the Muslim countries responded in different ways to this interaction with the West. All sections of Muslims did not respond in the same way. Some ruling classes, in order to preserve their privileges, resorted to Islamic identities to keep their downtrodden in subjugated conditions.

Indian feudal Muslim rulers and the downtrodden Muslims are examples of the varied responses to the colonial period. Here, while the poor and toiling sections joined the national movement based on secular principles, the landed classes resorted to politics in the garb of Islam—the Muslim League. The partition tragedy and the lining up of classes irrespective of their religion is a good pointer to the attitude of people. The feudal ruling classes did embrace Islamic identity to preserve their exalted position vis-à-vis the peasants and workers.

In Malaysia, British colonialism brought about a clear distinction between religion and state, with the "introduction of civil administration and a legal system distinct from the Islamic legal system and courts. At the same time, society also became more pluralistic as a result of massive immigration of non-Muslims, Chinese and Indians…" (Esposito and Voll 1996, 125). The Malay community, which was in majority, faced the choice of accepting a plural democracy, to accept multiculturalism.

> Initial British proposals of united Malay national identity became political issues as Malaysia moved towards independence in post-World War II period. Initial British proposals for a united Malay union, with equal citizenship for all, were rejected by Malays, who feared the growing population, economic power, and influence of Chinese and Indian communities, who enjoyed a higher economic and educational level than Malay Muslims. (ibid.)

In due course, Malay nationalism and Islam became the base of the leading opposition party. Islam and Malay culture got the place of primacy in the constitution, which at the time accorded the freedom of religion to people belonging to other faiths.

Greater was the influence of industrialization and modern education, more was the secularization process in those countries. Turkey and Egypt were amongst the ones where the Ulema was not the major power and secular governments could come into being. In many other Islamic countries, the Ulema and feudal forces became stronger in reaction to the hegemony of the Western powers. In the disintegrating Ottoman Empire, Mustafa Kemal Pasha, Atatürk, managed to keep his country free from the imperialist influence and also secularize it a great deal. Even after some of these countries became independent, the West often continued to control their economies, the oil, or other resources like the Suez Canal. When the British withdrew from India, they not only partitioned it, but also kept their economic and military interests intact. "In 1948 the Arabs of Palestine lost their homeland to the Zionists, who set up the Jewish secular state of Israel there, with the support of United Nations and the international community" (Armstrong 2002, 127). Many intellectuals of these countries also recognized the modern notions of Western values. Iranian intellectuals Mulkum Khan (1833–1908) and Aga Khan Kirmani urged Muslims to acquire Western education and replace sharia with a modern secular code, seeing this as the only route to progress. This was best exemplified in the ideas of Rifa'a al-Tahtawi (1801–1873), who was very impressed by the ideas of European enlightenment and equated those to *falsafah* (philosophy). Even before colonization became a phenomenon, many Islamic rulers tried to reform their administrations and societies. Some of these reforms were too rapid for those societies, and sometimes the use of brutality to impose these was intolerable for the population. Many of these reforms were superficial, not affecting the deeper societal relationships. This resulted in the adverse reaction from the ulema, "The ulama, who had experienced modernity as a shocking assault, became even more insular and closed their minds against new world that was coming into being in their country" (Armstrong 2002, 129).

The complex socioeconomic phenomenon shook the social relations of the society. The feudal values were cloaked as Islam persisted in different forms. As we have seen, feudalism in these countries had already adopted the modern social norms, which were nowhere close to the Islamic tenets. With the coming in of colonial rulers, and the social changes, modern education at places changed social equations. Since the modern values did not fully replace the feudal values, the emerging scenario became a mix of feudal values in the name of Islam and despotic rule and authoritarian structures. While many intellectuals tried to advocate for modern values arguing that they do not go against the teachings of Islam, the mullahs and the clergy, which had come to be in practice, and their protectors, the feudal elements, opposed the change in the garb of Islam. This dual use of Islam took the form of struggles and resulted in different streams within these countries. This also led to halfway houses between feudal and modern systems of political organization.

Interestingly, all the Muslim countries come in the zone of what is called as the Third World. Most of these countries are underdeveloped and still retain a large, feudal as well as semi-feudal social structure.

The economies of these countries depend, more or less, not without exceptions of course, either on sale of oil or on export of raw materials and agricultural products, primarily to the advanced industrial nations.

It is during the colonial era that Russia witnessed the Proletarian revolution. The revolution could not sustain, and gradually it got transformed into the rule of the communist party; later, the communist party rule got centralized in the central committee of the party, to be ultimately substituted by the authoritarian rule of its General Secretary, Joseph Stalin. This socialism came to be synonymous with the State-owned enterprises and centralized planning by the communist parties. Soviet Russia did provide an alternate pole to the imperialist West for quite some time. It was during this period that the two major power hegemonies on the scene and the third world countries could maneuver their space for social, economic, and cultural development. During this phase, the UN did exercise some moral authority. The Cold War era, with all its flaws, had a balance of power. During this era, the imperialism became more and more concentrated in the United States. The United States emerged as the major dominating power and it interfered everywhere under the garb of defense of freedom and democracy. The notion that was projected was the fear that if the United States did not intervene or take control of a particular area of the world, the Soviet Union, and communism, would fill the gap and destroy the democracy and freedom; so the United States must play the role of defender of the democracy of the world.

The so-called socialist system began with the Russian revolution. Most of the countries under the socialist system had come out from the clutches of the colonial powers. As a matter of fact, these were communist parties, which brought in bureaucratic regimes, and these ushered in the era of industrialization and state-controlled, centrally planned economies. Due to the weak industrial classes, the development of indigenous industrialization without State assistance was out of the question. Pakistan and many other states exemplify the fate of these States that could not industrialize and remained in the grip of colonial powers. India falls somewhere in between; the industrial class has contributed a bit to industrialization, but major, heavy industrialization came with the public sector and the State-controlled economy. The imperialists preferred States like Pakistan who could remain under their thumb and were averse to the development of native industrial structures.

Vietnam became the major symbol of imperialist lust to keep the colonies under control, and when France could not keep its grip, the United States tried its best (worst) to keep Vietnam under the tutelage of its army. The Vietnam policy of the United States was blatantly played under the banner of defense of democracy, the threat of evil communism. Vietnamese nationalism was too strong to be suppressed by the US might, and the killing of civilians in thousands also resulted in Viet Cong retaliating and killing some US soldiers. The death of the US soldiers resulted in public pressure, despite the heavy indoctrination by the US media and state machinery, with the result that the United States had to retreat, and Vietnam got its independence. The United States learnt the lesson of not meddling in colonies with one's own, army and that is what resulted in the training of Al Qaeda by the United States for the evacuation of Afghanistan occupied by the Soviet Union's army.

As such, these states were emerging from the clutches of feudal structures of society. With the collapse of the Soviet states, the hegemony of imperialist powers, now totally dominated by the United States, surpassed the worst types of hegemonies. Its dictates started becoming more and more focused on the enhancement of powers, and this also saw the serious erosion of the authority of the UN.

The era of national liberation saw many colonies becoming armed with political independence. But these were burdened by the economic domination of the imperialist powers. At the same time, the nation was not totally free from feudal structures and countries remained chained with premodern values. The independence of Muslim countries had many handicaps.

The American Agenda in West Asia and the Rise of Terrorism

The seeds of the present complex scenario and the rise of terrorism, as known at present, lie in the post-WW II era. This was a period when Soviet Russia stabilized as a powerful State and the United States emerged first as the leader and then as the sole capitalist superpower, the imperialist power. The world had two major superpowers—the United States and the USSR. The destructive power of weapons, more so nuclear weapons, had become obvious all around the globe. It was by and large common understanding that major wars between the superpowers should be avoided. And their clash of interests did lead to showdowns, but these did not conflagrate into the war. The contradictory interests of the superpowers kept manifesting themselves as the Cold War, and shadowboxing, which manifested in the skirmishes in other countries. The rivalry between superpowers plunged the world into suffering and clashes. These clashes also laid part of the foundation of the terrorism that was to rise after the 1970s. The Cold War symbolized indirect battle rather than the direct confrontation of superpowers. "With the beginning of cold war, the weapon of the weak, terrorism became the weapon of the powerful nations. Terrorism became the expression of cold war" (Karan 1997, 98).

During the Cold War era, the United States was too glad to shake hands with terrorists or to promote those set of terrorists who could work in favor of its interests, that is, against the USSR. It is through terrorism that the United States launched the anti-USSR attacks, and also wars against the other socialist states. It was in the backdrop of the Vietnam War that the United States was forced to adopt this policy. The United States realized after the Vietnam War that direct intervention would not be acceptable to the US public because the loss of lives of the US soldiers the US was totally against the policy of directly attacking other countries. As per Ronald Regan, the State had authorized the CIA to use any means to destabilize the socialist states.

> With the aim of destabilizing or overthrowing the socialist governments or the one's sympathetic to USSR, CIA fully supported, through financial, military political and diplomatic aid to the separatist, counterrevolutionary rebel groups e.g. Unitar in Angola, Contras in Nicaragua. Through secret military coups and political assassinations (e.g. Chile's Allende) it tried to achieve its goals. It even went on to undertake direct military interventions. (Tripathi et al. 2002, 33)

The United States used the language of saving the world from communism, making the world safe for democracy, and defending freedom. Some of the policies of the United States in smaller countries tell the real truth of the intent of US policies. In Dominican Republic, after the murder of President Trujillo, Juan Bosch was elected as the President.

He brought about total social reform for the welfare of the people. These reforms adversely affected the interests of the United States in this country. The military overthrew him, and after a formal motion of objecting to the overthrow of a democratically elected government, it supported the military regime, which in turn restored the interests of the United States. The result of the US*supported military takeover was "death squads, torture, repression, an increase in poverty and malnutrition for the mass of population, slave labor conditions, vast emigration, and outstanding opportunities for US investors, whose control over the economy reached new heights" (Chomsky 1985). A similar story was repeated in Guatemala, where Jacobo Arbenz was elected as President in 1951. He went in for land reforms and tried to expropriate unused land from United Fruit Company after due compensation; this was seen as a 'communist game', endorsing the civil rights of communists. Under the pretext of stopping the communist takeover, the good old CIA overthrew the democratically elected government of Guatemala and restored military rule (Cogswell 1996, 131). Chomsky adds, "Land reform was repealed, its beneficiaries dispossessed, peasants cooperatives were dissolved, literacy program was halted, the economy collapsed, the labor unions were destroyed and killings began" (Chomsky 1985, 131). The same pattern repeated ad infinitum, the US interference in Nicaragua being on the same lines. The seeds of terrorism, which was to come up in the Middle East in a big way, were also sown by policies like these.

On the other hand, the USSR also openly supported the rebel groups opposing the tyrants and dictators supported by the United States. The United States went on to build its army and naval bases in Saudi Arabia, Turkey, Diego Garcia, Philippines, Japan, and South Korea. The United States. They openly supported the states of Indonesia, Chile, Mexico, Honduras, and Costa Rica to suppress the communist rebellions.

Barring Indonesia, Malaysia, Pakistan, and Bangladesh, most of the Islamic countries are located in West Asia and East Africa. India also has a substantial Muslim population. The area where terrorism prevails is West Asia, the zone that is rich in oil. Also, almost all Islamic countries are situated in the Third World.

> Most of these countries are underdeveloped and still retain, by and large, feudal or semi feudal social structures. The economies of these countries

like Saudi Arabia, Kuwait etc. have become quite rich with high per capita income due to many fold increase in oil prices after Arab Israeli war of 1973. But other Islamic countries continue to be poor and backward. Even the oil rich countries are, scientifically, technologically, industrially and socially speaking quite backward. (Engineer 1994, 150)

This has resulted in massive changes and has also made them vulnerable to US influence, pressure, or subjugation on one or the other pretext. It is no coincidence that Islamic fundamentalism thrives more in this region, in contrast to the impression that the whole Islamic world is a fertile ground for fundamentalism.

As such, the fundamentalist movement has gained momentum in countries such as Pakistan, Iran, Libya, and Saudi Arabia. In countries such as Afghanistan, Iraq, South Yemen, Syria, and Algeria, either Marxist or left-leaning governments were in power until recently. During the left-leaning regimes, people in these countries did follow Islam in their lives, but in the matters of state policies, traditional values did not play a direct role. In Indonesia and Malaysia, there are militant Islamic parties. The formation of Israel was the major source of conflict. The other cause of conflict was the overt desire of the United States to control the oil resources of this region. The major threat shifted to West Asia. While the United States kept controlling other countries, expanding its economic empire to West Asia. The US policy was and remains to be the major cause of the turmoil in this area. It was also to see the rise of terrorism in its most dangerous form after the decade of the 1980s. The conflict first came with the Eisenhower Doctrine, named after the then US President. It simply meant that the United States would give economic and military aid to the countries in this region to "protect them from international communism." The United States continued to arm Israel to the teeth. It kept sending armies to maintain the pro-Western governments.

The Palestine Issue

The events of the Middle East had their roots chiefly in the Israel–Palestine problem. The rise of Arab nationalism was opposed on the grounds that it is a sign of the increase of Soviet influence and there is threat to freedom due to the rise of communism. Western countries were determined to retain their control over the Middle East for oil.

The problem of Israel was to add to the intensity of conflict in this area. Jewish immigration was another area of discomfort in this region. The UN had agreed to partition the Palestine into the Jewish state of Israel and Arab Palestine. However, even before the partition could be affected, Britain, which was holding Palestine as a mandate, withdrew in 1948. The United States immediately recognized the formation of the Jewish state of Israel. This is referred to by Israelis as the War of Independence, and Palestinians call it Nabka—the catastrophe. During this war, more than half of the Palestinian population of 1,380,000 were driven off their homeland by the Israeli army.

> Though Israel officially claimed that the majority of refugees fled and were not expelled, it still refused to allow them to return, as a UN resolution demanded shortly after the 1948 war. Thus the Israeli land was obtained through ethnic cleansing of the indigenous Palestinian inhabitants. (Reinhart 2003, 7)

This was just the beginning of a series of Israel actions that were to plunge the Middle East in to darkness. It was the beginning of the hegemonic Israel designs, duly backed by the United States all through. This was followed by the Arab–Israel war in which Israel won. Over a million Arab Palestinians had to leave their home and hearth and become refugees. In 1967, following a war with three neighboring Arab counties, Israel conquered and occupied the West Bank (from Jordan), the Gaza Strip, and Sinai Peninsula (from Egypt), and Golan Heights (from Syria). Barring the Sinai Peninsula, the other territories are still with Israel. This resulted in a fresh wave of almost 0.25 million refugees coming in from the West Bank and the Gaza Strip. About 3 million Palestinians still live in these areas under Israeli occupation surrounded by Israeli settlements built on their lands. Occupation does lead to a complex sociopolitical phenomenon.

> A state governing a hostile population of 1.5–2 million foreigners [number of the Palestinians in the occupied territories at the time] is bound to become a Shin Bet (Security Service) state with all that this implies for the spirit of education, freedom of speech and through democracy. Israel will be infected with corruption, characteristic of any colonial regime. The administration will have to deal with the suppression of an Arab protest

movement on the one hand, and with the acquisition of Arab quislings on the other.… The army, which has been so far a people's army will degenerate as well by becoming an occupation army, and its officers turned into military governors, will not differ from military governors elsewhere in the world. (Leibowitz 1969)

After the 1967 war, the US–Israeli nexus became thicker. In 1982, the Israeli army destroyed the Palestine Liberation Army, which had developed in the Palestinian refugee camps in Lebanon and taken permanent control of southern Lebanon, which borders Israel. Israeli society did recognize that the attack on Lebanon was a failure, but its army continued to occupy Lebanon till May 2000. At the same time, Israeli occupation of the land in 1967 continued undisturbed.

Israeli society realized that its military occupation was a heavy price to pay after the first Palestinian uprising. Many in the Israeli society felt morally uncomfortable about the occupation.

On the Palestinian side, the struggle for independence was also based—for the first time—on explicit recognition of Israel's right to exist (in its pre-1967 borders). As we shall see, the Intifada meeting of Palestinian National Council in 1988 called for the partition of historical Palestine into two independent states. The struggle against occupation became joint Israeli–Palestinian struggle, with many Israeli opposition groups demonstrating in the territories, or inviting Palestinian leaders to speak at teach-ins in Israeli universities. (Reinhart 2003, 10)

The Oslo Accord requiring Israel to withdraw from the occupied territories was signed in Washington, D.C. in 1993. It was believed that Israel would withdraw after this accord and occupation would come to an end. As it turns out, this accord has been turned into one more sophisticated way of keeping the occupation going as far as Israel is concerned. Israel, at its aggressive worst, aims to retrieve more from the Palestine state. Large sections of Israel's population seem to be tired of war; the present leadership is driven by the goal to occupy more land and to get more resources. It is remarkable how Israel has been violating all the UN resolutions with impunity and is thoroughly backed by the United States in all its goals. It is so because at a deeper level, the goals of the United States and Israel run parallel.

The Israel–Palestine struggle became the Israel–Arab struggle right from the word go. Taking advantage of this, the United States set up military bases in the Gulf region. The central aim of these was to ensure that the USSR should not be able to enter the oil-rich zone. It was projected as the defense of the region from communism. However, more than defense of the region, it was defense of the Sheikhs who were ruthlessly controlling and ruling those regions, and, of course, the US interests in oil. Fareed Zakaria, Editor of *Newsweek*, points out, "Majority of Americans think that Arabs should feel grateful to the US for the protection it offered Kuwait and Saudi Arabia. Contrary to this, majority of Arabs think that US has protected the royal families of Saudi Arabia and Kuwait" (Zakaria 2001).

The United States started playing the same role as Britain was playing before the war. The difference was that by now Arab nationalism had come up, which saw the role of the United States in protecting the interests of Israel and depriving the Palestinians from the right of self-determination. The fact that Israel is able to carry out unilateral, illegal actions backed by US support is evident to all, and a painful truth for the Arabs. Over a period of time, this has resulted in anti-US sentiments. The Palestinian movement is fairly old and based on secular principles. It was supported by the USSR. Israel's unchecked, intimidating, and rising power has given a serious jolt to the Palestinian movement.

Terrorism from amongst Palestinians began in 1967 as a consequence of the intense frustration due to their defeat in the aggression by Israel. The Palestine Liberation Organization Board got recognition all over in 1964 as a secular umbrella for various organizations, whose aim was to form an independent Palestine. The 1967 defeat at the hands of Israel came as a big shock and dejection, and it was felt that Israel could not be confronted in war. It is after this that sections of the PLO started tilting toward terror tactics. Yasser Arafat's Al-Fatah joined the PLO in 1958 and assumed the leadership of this organization; he succeeded in broadening it and went on to become the symbol of the struggle of the Palestinians. The PLO got recognition across the board, while Israel due to its high-handedness and regular violation of UN norms remained isolated; but at the same time it went on to become stronger due to the backing of the United States.

As such the acts of terrorism in middle east were resorted to by Israelis. The secret agents of Israeli army and police undertook terrorist acts including hijacking of civilian planes and ships, abductions for ransom…selective killings, carnage and bombing the civilian targets" (Tripathi et al. 2002, 55). As per Noam Chomsky, "Israeli actions are never regarded as terrorism, they are justified by being labeled as actions in self-defense. (Chomsky 1986, 3)

It is remarkable that despite serious provocations the Palestinian organization while resorting to terrorism did not target the citizens. The organizations which did resort to terrorism during this phase were Popular Front for the Liberation of Palestine (PFLP; a group founded by George Habash, who was one of the founders of the PLO but separated from it in 1993 due to differences), Abu Nidal (a radical terrorist group involved in many a terrorist attacks in the 1980s, now weakened), and Popular Front for the Liberation of Palestine-General Command (PFLP-GC; opposed to the PLO, focused more on armed attacks). By and large, with a few exceptions, the PLO remained restrained as far as violent activities were concerned. A terrorist organization which the breakaways from PLO, by and large avoided the killing of civilians. One of the exceptions to this has been the terrorist attack in the Munich Olympics, where Israeli players were kidnapped and killed.

Overall, due to the dominating and military might of Israel, the Arabs have surrendered a lot of land.

[T]here has run a clear and to me, unnecessary line of Arab capitulation, by which Israel has achieved all of its tactical and strategic objectives at the expense of nearly every proclaimed principle of Arab and Palestinian nationalism and struggle. Thus Israel has gained recognition, legitimacy and acceptance from Arabs without in effect conceding sovereignty over the Arab land, including annexed Jerusalem, captured illegally by war. (Said 1995, xxi)

The situation has been in favor of illegitimate Israeli intentions.

In the present situation Israel has managed to convince the Arabs and in particular the exhausted Palestinian leadership that equality is impossible, that peace only on Israeli terms and those dictated by US is possible. Years of unsuccessful wars, empty bellicosity, immobilized population, and incompetence and corruption at every level bled the life out of our societies, already crippled by a total absence of participatory democracy and the hope that goes with it. (ibid.)

Afghanistan

Afghanistan has been the eye of the storm for the past three decades. This country situated to the northwest of India is located at a crucial geographical position; to top that, it is also close to the vast oil resources of the Caspian Sea. It is a Muslim majority state, with 99 percent of the population being Muslims. It has been predominantly a tribal society, with Pashtuns, Tajiks, and Uzbeks being the major ones. There is also a small percentage of Kazaks, Kirgiz, and Turkmen. Afghanistan has a federal structure in which the state governments control all affairs barring defense, finance, and external affairs. Zoroastrian, Buddhism, and Islam are the major religions. Afghanistan had close links with India and Pakistan. Many Indian kings, including the Sikhs, have ruled parts of this country. Islam spread greatly in the country in medieval times, during the rule of Ghazni, Ghori, Lodi, and other Mughal rulers. It was also an important center of Buddhism; Bamiyan Buddha's statues were witness to the rich cultural heritage of Afghanistan.

Ahmad Shah Abdali, who brought together the smaller states, laid the foundation of modern Afghanistan. In the 19th century, Russian and British expansionists eyed Afghanistan. Afghanistan went into war with Britain twice. Later, Russia and Britain both carved out some areas of influence in Afghanistan for themselves. After the second Anglo-Afghan war, Britain came to control Afghanistan, despite which there was there was a strong opposition toward British empire. After the third Anglo-Afghan war, Amanullah Khan succeeded in controlling Afghanistan and it became independent on August 19, 1919.

Amanullah ruled for nearly a decade, and he was very different from the earlier rulers. He abandoned the isolationist foreign policy and charted the course of striking diplomatic relations with many countries. Influenced by Atatürk of Turkey, he also tried to modernize Afghanistan in the direction of secularism. Reforms amongst women, abolition of *burqa* (veil), and starting of coeducation schools were some of the major reforms brought in by him. The conservative sections had lot of appeal within the country; they started opposing these moves and challenged the power of Amanullah, who had to renounce power in 1929. This led to control over Kabul by Bacha Sakka of the Tajik community, who by adopting fundamentalist policies succeeded in pleasing the conservatives. He started campaigns against idol worship and closed down coeducational schools. Pashtuns were unable to accept him as the ruler. Amanullah's nephew Mohammed Nadir Shah succeeded in overthrowing his rule and captured Kabul. A supporter of Amanullah Khan killed him.

Nadir Shah's son Muhammad Zahir Shah became the ruler of Afghanistan; the same Zahir Shah has been playing a prominent role currently. Zahir Shah was to take over after the ouster of Taliban. He was the choice of the Western powers, but the local people felt that he had not been concerned with the Afghan issues for long. He ruled for 40 long years. Initially, his uncle guided him. From 1953, he relieved his uncle of his responsibilities and appointed Daud Khan as his Prime Minister. Daud Khan's demand for a separate Pashtun state annoyed Pakistan and it jeopardized the trade interests of Afghanistan due to which he had to be removed from prime ministership. Zahir Shah did try to reduce the hold of the royal family on the state administration. He was keen to modernize Afghanistan and bring in modern political culture, and socioeconomic pattern. The social and political changes being brought about from the top were aimed at improving the social structure while using traditional symbolism. Zahir Shah laid the foundation of modern universities in conjunction with advisers from Europe. The 1931 Constitution was changed over to one aimed at bringing in the educated classes into the new power equations. The new constitution was ratified by the liberal Loya Jirga (Assembly). This constitution had provisions whereby the executive, judiciary, and legislative wings were separated.

This also paved the way for the formation of political parties and freedom of press. Unfortunately, the new assembly Wolesi Jirga's members were tribal chiefs, feudal, clerics, and conservative elements who were unaware of the modern tasks of legislatures. This resulted in the power continuing to be centered in the hands of the king. All said and done, these were progressive measures and improved the lot of the Afghani people, more so the women. The severe drought of 1972–1973 resulted in a drastic change in the system of governance. As Zahir Shah went to Europe, his government was overthrown and Daud Khan usurped the throne.

During the liberal political regime of Zahir Khan, many liberal sections of society started seeing the importance of Marxist Communist ideas for their country. With the help of Soviet Russia, they started looking forward to a communist regime in Afghanistan. They formed the People's Democratic Party of Afghanistan (PDPA) in 1965. "People's Democratic Party of Afghanistan, which had a strong base in army and air force, carried out a coup d'état in 1978, toppling the corrupt regime of Daud. People welcomed the change. PDPA was initially popular. It pledged important social reforms and democracy" (Ali 2001). Later, this party got divided into Khalq and Parcham factions.

> The leader of Khalk faction was Nur Muhammad Taraqui and Parcham group leader was Babrak Karmal. This was the first setback to Communist movement in Afghanistan. Due to worsening economic situation in Afghanistan Daud Khan's people's anger against him was on the rise. The pressure of the internal situation of Afghanistan forced the two factions to come together…on April 27 1978 a communist coup overthrew the regime of Daud Khan and for the first time a Communist party came to power. (Tripathi et al. 2002, 126)

The changes in Afghanistan were massive and progressive. The opposition to these changes from the conservative sections started being repressed once the Pol Pot section within the party emerged victorious.

After the communists came to power, the mullahs and conservative elements declared *jihad* against the regime. Youth started being trained as mujahideen to overthrow the communist government. The United States also took a serious note of this; in the times to come, it was to play a central role in the overthrow of the communist government. It started providing arms, ammunitions, and money in big amounts to the mujahideen. The efforts of the United States were supplemented by Pakistan, Saudi Arabia, and some Gulf countries. The communist regime started implementing the land reforms on a large scale. This hit the interests of landlords and the mullahs who started supporting the mujahideen. The rebellion started from East Afghanistan and spread to important cities. The mujahideen succeeded in paralyzing the administration. Hafizullah Amin overthrew Nur Muhammad Taraki and came to power. The hold of PDPA in the rural areas started declining. By 1979, the communist government became very weak, ruling only six of the 29 states of

Afghanistan; consequently, the reform efforts of the communist party suffered a setback.

To think that the United States stepped up the interference in Afghanistan, as a retaliation against USSR intervention, is a travesty of the truth. As such,

> Secret American air to opponents of pro-Soviet regime in Kabul had begun before the Soviet army invaded Afghanistan. CIA and state department documents seized during embassy takeover in Tehran reveal that the US had begun quietly meeting Afghan-rebel representatives in Pakistan in April 1979, eight months before Soviet military intervention. This much was confirmed by Zhigniew Brzezinski, President Carter's national security advisor, in a later interview with Paris-based *Le Nouvel Observateur* (January 15–21, 1998). (Mamdani 2005, 123)

Due to the attacks of the mujahideen, Soviet Russia decided to send its army to Afghanistan, and PDPA's (Parcham) Babrak Karmal became the new President. The unpleasant civil war underwent a transformation at this point of time. The Soviet armies were seen as foreign armies. This enabled the US-funded mujahideen, the holy warriors, to step up their activities. The US officials got a bigger chance to court and manipulate the mujahideens; they were told, "Allah is on your side."

> Meanwhile US decided to destabilize the regime by arming the ultra-religious tribes and by using the Pakistani army as a conduit to help the religious extremists. The Americans were laying bear trap and Soviet leadership fell into it. They sent the Red army to topple Amin and sustain PDPA regime by force. This further exacerbated the crisis and United States gave a call for a jihad against communism. (Ali 2001)

John Cooley, in his account of this phase of the Cold War (Cooley 2002, 209), states that the Chinese not only helped with the provision of weapons, but also extended the help of volunteers, whose services were paid for by the CIA. Tariq Ali quotes Ahmad Mansur of Muslim, who spotted Israeli advisors in the war against Soviet occupation (ibid., 209).

The United States intensified its intervention in Afghanistan. The CIA, through Pakistan's ISI, started to intervene. With the Soviet intervention, different battalions joined the mujahideen.

> In 1980, the US spent $8 billion in Afghanistan to defeat the Soviets. Pakistan introduced the idea of creating an International Brigade to fight the war, encouraging thousands of Muslims to join, and even put pressure on Saudis to send a prince to join the war. In 1986, CIA chief William Casey persuaded Congress to send military supplies to these people. Laden, a rich Saudi, arrived in Peshawar and was welcomed by Pakistan and United States as he was to lead Saudi contingent. (Ali 2001)

At the height of war, there were 100,000 Soviet ground troops in Afghanistan. It presented the United States with the opportunity to avenge its Vietnam debacle. Regan formulated the offensive against communism at a global level and went all the way to promote Islamic terrorism, as it is known today. The United States had suffered the effects of direct intervention and so wanted to fight the battle through proxy. Wahabi Islam, regional geopolitical strategies, and interests of Saudi Arabia and Pakistan were used to the hilt to attack Soviet forces in Afghanistan. This CIA operation was a long bloody intervention to 'save democracy and freedom'.

Close cooperation developed between the CIA and the ISI and the United States pumped in millions of dollars as aid to support the *jihadi* activities. Both the United States and Pakistan had no interest in negotiated settlement and they recruited the most rabid Islamists as mujahideen and gave them the most sophisticated weapons in abundance. This was converted into a global war against communism. The result was that the region became full of recruits coming from all over the world and being trained in the CIA–ISI training centers. One Sheikh, Abdul Azam, was to play an important role in recruitment, "A Palestinian theologian who had a doctorate in Islamic law from Al Azhar University, in Jiddah, where one of his students was Osama bin Laden" (Lawrence Wright, "The New Yorker." quoted in Mamdani 2005, 126–127). He traveled all over the globe with CIA patronage and appeared on Saudi TV. He was to be one of the founders of Hamas. His *jihad* meant killing the Russians and striving for martyrdom.

> CIA was determined to create one (jihad) in the service of a contemporary political objective.... US organized the Afghan Jihad and that informed its central objective: to unite a billion Muslim worldwide in a holy war, a crusade, against the Soviet Union, on the soil of Afghanistan. (ibid., 128)

With Regan's second term in office, all the brakes on the support to this effort, if at all, were released, and the United States launched a full-fledged war on Soviet forces. Regan signed a National Security Decision Directive 166 authorizing moves that "stepped-up covert military aid to the mujahideen, and it made clear that the secret Afghan war had a new goal: to defeat Soviet troops in Afghanistan through covert action and encourage Soviet withdrawal" (quoted in The Redefined War: Rashid 2000, 129–30).

The Saudi government also played an important role in funding the training of the *jihadis*.

> All the money and arms were channeled through Pakistan's ISI. The Saudis boosted their religious and anti-communist radio broadcasts into Afghanistan and central Asia. Arms were being purchased on the international market with Saudi money and CIA was flying them from Dharan to Islamabad. Ten thousand tons of arms and ammunition were going through the channel each year. By 1985 this rose to 65000 tons. (Lokshahi Hakk Sangathan 2001, 13)

The war as redefined now was taken over by William Casey, the CIA chief. He outlined three significant measures, out of which two were taken up. One was to step up US involvement in the mujahideen war by providing US advisors and new weapons like stringer missiles. The second one of extending the war into the society territory of Tajikistan and Uzbekistan could not be implemented due to USSR threat to attack Pakistan. The third one was to increase the recruitment of radical Islamists from all over the world. All this made it a Muslim affair worldwide and it used the Muslim institutions as conduits for these actions.

Zia-ul-Haq, under whose regime the military–mullah complex strengthened under US patronage, was supported to the hilt by the CIA, which ran several programs to keep him in power. "Numerous schools were established in 1985 to train fighters in weapon usage. Two week courses in antitank and anti-aircraft guns, mine laying and lifting, demolitions, urban warfare and sabotage were offered for thousands of fighters" (ibid., 13). The CIA employed a clever ploy in integrating teachings of Islam with military guerilla warfare. The sum and substance of this ideological training was that Islam was an integrated sociopolitical ideology, that holy Islam was being violated by atheistic Soviet troops, the communist government, so it was the religious duty of the people of Afghanistan and Muslims all over the world to assert the independence of Islam by overthrowing the Soviet-sponsored regime in Afghanistan. Since the ISI was the major conduit of this *jihadi* training, it became an inflated powerful body within the state of Pakistan.

A journalist from Pakistan, Ahmad Rashid, points out that Osama started traveling to Pakistan bringing the Arab donations for this *jihad*. In 1982, he decided to settle in Peshawar and

> ...in 1986 he worked as a major contractor to build large CIA funded project, the Khost tunnel complex deep under mountains close to the Pakistani border. The Khosht complex housed a major arms depot, a training facility and a medical center for mujahideen. It is the Khost complex that President Clinton decided in 1998 to bomb with Tamahawk cruise missiles. It is also in the Khost complex...that the US later fought Al Qaeda remnants in its own Afghan war. (Mamdani 2005, 133)

The use of Islam, *jihad*, and related Islamic institutions was the strategy adopted by the United States to counter the left-wing regime in Afghanistan. And this was to be the pivot around which the US policy of destroying communism revolved. This anticommunist campaign was mixed with religious emotions; the ones associated with Islam, were misused blatantly. Madrassas were used to give politico-religious training to Islamic guerillas. The curriculum of these madrassas was so designed that "predominant themes were that Islam was a complete sociopolitical ideology, that holy Islam was being violated by atheistic Soviet troops, and that the Islamic people of Afghanistan should reassert their independence by overthrowing the leftist Afghan regime propped up by Moscow" (Dilip Hiro, quoted in Chossudovsky 2001). These madrassas taught that the Islamic revolution in Afghanistan would be a precursor of such Islamic revolutions in other parts of the world. Many students from Central Asia started getting such training in Deoband madrassas in Pakistan, with free lodging and boarding; some of these were later to be a part of the Taliban. Pervez Hoodbhoy gives interesting examples of the questions asked in a third-grade book. He writes, "One group of mujahideen attack 50 Russian soldiers. In that attack 20 Russians are killed. How many Russians fled?" (Hoodbhoy 2002, 7–8). These government and private madrassas took care of the indoctrination and the military camps provided training in warfare techniques. The University of Nebraska under a $50 million USAID (United States Agency for International Development) grant supported books promoting violence and acts of terror. There were many types of madrassas giving similar indoctrination. The military training was given in army camps. Over 80,000 mujahideen were trained and at least 10,000 received military training, while the number of mujahideen who actually fought was much less.

> Tariq Ali gives an estimate of 2500 madrassas with an annual crop of 225000 students, many of whom had been taught literacy in primers that stated that the Urdu letter tay stood for *tope* (cannon), kaaf for Kalashnikov, khay for khoon (blood) and jeem for jihad. (Mamdani 2005, 138)

CIA training focused on how to produce and spread violence formation of private militias, capable of creating terror. The *jihad* was also financed through drug trade. The Afghan people were levied to produce opium which was sent back in ships which were bringing armaments. The ships were protected from being searched by ISI papers. The nature of mujahideen groups was diverse. They were deliberately decentralized around some differences.

Thousands of young Muslims from all over the world were trained as mujahideens. "Largely out of sight of the world, in training camps in Afghanistan and Pakistan, something akin to radical Islamic foreign legion was taking shape" (Rashid 2000, 44). Many of these continued to receive their training even after the withdrawal of Soviet troops. "The real damage the CIA did was not the providing of arms and money but privatization of information about how to produce and spread violence— the formation of private militias—capable of creating terror" (Mamdani 2005, 138).

One of the dangerous faces of CIA operations was to fund the terrorist activities through opium trade. They developed a whole chain of trade in which, to begin with, mujahideen forced the cultivation of opium as revolutionary tax, "As the Mujahideen guerillas seized territory inside Afghanistan, they ordered peasants to plant opium as revolutionary tax" (McCoy 1997, 24–27). One of the 'bright' plans of the CIA was to load the opium in containers which were bringing in arms and ammunition;

and on return, when the containers were empty, they were filled with opium and sealed; it was exempted from customs.

With the rise of the Third World, the United States got alarmed as it foresaw the rise in the area of influence of the Soviet Union. It went on to formulate a policy to counter the Soviet influence by any means possible. Promoting the Muslim right wing and training Muslim youth into Islamic warriors, *jihadis* were totally a planning of the CIA. By making Afghanistan a theater of major offensive, the war became global due to the label of the war, *jihad*, its identification with Islam, its goal to beat back the godless communists, and also taking advantage of the fact that the Russian army did come into Afghanistan. "As it stretched through near a decade of Regan presidency, the Afghan war turned into bloodiest regional conflict in the world" (Mamdani 2005, 120).

The mujahideen infiltrated the Afghan army. By 1985, they became very strong, with the help of the United States and Gulf countries; they formed a strong base in Kabul and started attacking the government establishment. The Pakistani army thought it would help *jihad* if the Saudi prince led the struggle, but volunteers from that quarter were not forthcoming. Instead, the Saudi regime suggested Osama bin Laden to the CIA. He was approved, recruited, trained, and sent to Afghanistan, where he fought well. In one action, bin Laden led his men to attack a mixed school (boys and girls) and killed all the teachers. The United States watched this approvingly.

> From 1980 to 1985 America's secret service CIA and many a Muslim countries provided heavy economic aid to Mujahideens. According to one estimate this amounted to 2 billion dollars. Osama bin Laden was part of this as a US operative against the Soviet forces. During 1985–87 US provided seventy thousand tons of ammunition, including the stringer missiles. (Tripathi et al. 2002, 128)

The role of the United States in promoting mujahideen was most blatant. In an article he wrote for *Dawn*, Pakistani political thinker and activist Eqbal Ahmad draws our attention to an American television image from 1985. On White House lawns, President Ronald Regan is introducing, with great fanfare, a group of Afghan men, all leaders of the mujahideen, to the media: "These gentlemen are the moral equivalents of American founding fathers" (Mamdani 2005, 119).

Mujahideen were too powerful to be defeated. Due to ill health, Babrak Karmal stepped down and Najibullah became the head of the government. He declared ceasefire and released all the political prisoners. Soviet armies were defeated and they withdrew. With Soviet withdrawal, the United States relaxed its pressure through the CIA, but Pakistan continued its intervention. The ISI had played the conduit for the Saudi money to mujahideen. Pakistan has been scared of the demand of Pashtunistan, which will affect its own territory; half of the claimed Pashtunistan falls in the boundaries of Pakistan. Pakistan continued to help mujahideen in their offensive against the Najibullah government. Due to differences with the Army General, Abdul Rashid Dostum, Najibullah stepped down, leaving the power in hands of Burhanuddin Rabbani. The differing factions kept fighting each other; the civil war resulted in heavy casualties.

The United States had multiple goals in the Afghan war. To counter the local Iranian revolution and the Soviet intervention, it made regional alliances with Pakistan and Iraq. To counter the Islamist social movements, it encouraged the intelligence agencies of Saudi Arabia and Pakistan to promote anti-Shia–Sunni doctrines, the chief amongst these were the Wahabi doctrine from Saudi Arabia and Deobandi doctrine from Pakistan. The CIA also gave armaments to these groups depending on their strategic importance. As per Ahmad Rashid,

> When CIA funneled arms to Afghan Mujahideen via Pakistan's ISI, the ISI gave preference to radical Afghan Islamic parties—which could more easily be turned into engine of anti-Soviet jihad—and pushed aside moderate Afghan nationalist and Islamic parties. At that time CIA made no objections to this policy. (Jihad by Ahmad Rashid, 210, cited in Mamdani 2005, 155)

Taliban was the outcome of the mujahideen groups, trained in radical Islam and army warfare. Taliban arose from the US war against Russia in Afghanistan.

Pakistan continued its intervention in Afghanistan. It sent Taliban (students), trained in its seminaries, with the open support of army. Taliban's Islam is a virulent, sectarian, ultra-puritanical one, influenced by Wahabism, which is the official religion of Saudi Arabia. Saudi religious instructors trained Taliban.

While we will return to it later, it needs to be underlined that during this part of the Cold War era,the United States used the most retrograde and orthodox Islam to fight against the communist regime, the alternate of the superpower in the world. The Iranian revolution of Ayatollah Khomeini had a profound effect on the US policies in the region.

> Prior to it, America saw the world in rather simple terms: on one side was Soviet Union and militant third world nationalism, which America regarded as a Soviet tool; on the other side was political Islam, which America considered an unqualified ally in the struggle against Soviet union. Thus US supported Sarekat-I-Islam against Sukarno in Indonesia, the Jamat-I-Islami against Zulfiqar Ali Bhutto in Pakistan, and the society of Muslim Brothers against Nasser in Egypt. The expectation that political Islam would provide a local buffer against secular nationalism was also broadly shared by U.S. allies within the region, from Israel to conservative Arab regimes. (Mamdani 2005, 120–21)

Israel and the United States hoped to use militant Islam to keep their hold in the region. Israel first promoted Hamas before the first intifada with the hope to drive a wedge amongst the Palestinians, but later the same Hamas played an anti-Israeli role.

As a result of the way the war against Russian forces was fought, through the radical Islamists, later, the radical Islamists prevailed, moderate groups of Islam had no place in the future power structure, and Taliban, the most radical wing of these, emerged as the leaders in the power struggle which followed the retreat of the Russian forces.

Iraq

Iraq, earlier known as Mesopotamia, was part of Ottoman the Empire from the 16th century to 1918. It was divided into three provinces: Mosul (predominantly Kurdish) in the north, Baghdad (predominantly Sunni Arab) in the center, and Basra (predominantly Shiite Arab) in the south. With the fall of the Ottoman Empire, British and French governments undertook projects (railroads, Suez Canal, etc.) in the region; as a result, the government of the region became heavily indebted to the French and British banks. Britain was the direct ruler of Egypt, Sudan, and the Persian Gulf, while France was the dominant power in Lebanon and Syria. As seen above, Iran was divided between Russia and British areas of influence. Imperialist powers were on the lookout to carve out their areas of influence from the Ottoman Empire. Britain did realize that the oil wealth of the region may be crucial in future and started investing in oil companies in the region (e.g., Anglo-Persian Oil Company with 51 percent British stake).

Having this in mind, right at the beginning of WW I, Britain occupied Baghdad and Mosul. Britain promised the Arabs that it would support their independence, while also maintaining that Baghdad and Basra would be special zones of influences of the British. At the same time, in a contradictory arrangement with France (Sykes–Picot Agreement of 1916), it committed that Mosul would go to France and other two would go to Britain. Czarist Russia was to be compensated by giving territory in the northeast of Turkey as per this agreement. With Bolsheviks coming to power, they published this secret treaty making the Arabs realize the treachery of colonial powers.

The British betrayed the Arabs; France got the mandate for Syria and Lebanon, while Britain was to control Palestine and Iraq. Britain also controlled the Mosul region, in return for conceding French control in Lebanon and Syria. With Britain controlling Iraq, a revolt which soon became widespread broke out in Iraq and Britain suppressed it ruthlessly. This revolt right from the beginning shook the British who decided to put up a facade for their rule. Curzon, the foreign secretary, wanted in the Arab territories an

> Arab façade ruled and administered under British guidance and controlled by native Mohammedan and as far as possible, by an Arab staff…There should be no actual incorporation of conquered territory in the dominions of the conquers, but the absorption should be veiled by such constitutional fictions as a protectorate, a spree of influence…The British high commissioner proclaimed Emir Faisal I, belonging to Hashemite family of Mecca, which had ever been expelled from the French mandate of Syria, as the King of Iraq. The puppet Faisal promptly signed a treaty of alliance with Britain that largely reproduced the terms of mandate. This roused such strong nationalist protest that cabinet was forced to resign, and British high commissioner assumed dictatorial powers for several years. Nationalist leaders were deported from the country on a wide scale. (Research Unit for Political Economy, *Analytical Monthly Review*, May 2003, 22–23)

The British drafted a constitution for Iraq and gave quasi-dictatorial powers to the king. Despite the popular protest, the British went on to give more and more powers to their oil companies on the Iraqi oil. In the games which the imperialist powers were playing, Kurds were the worst sufferers whose territory got divided by the imperial powers into southern Turkey, northern Iraq, and northwest Iran.

> The terms of concession, covering virtually the entire country until the year 2000, were outrageous. Payment was four shillings (one fifth of British Pound) per ton of oil produced. For this extraordinary giveaway, the puppet king Faisal received a personal present of $40,000. It was this concession that oil corporations, for half a century thereafter, would fight to defend as their 'legitimate' right. (ibid., 23)

With the decline of Britain as the colonial power and the ascendance of the United States, the Unite States staked claim in the oil in the region.

Iraq got its independence from the British in 1932, thanks to its sustained struggle against the colonial rule. But treaties were extracted by Britain which ensured its continued economic interests, 'close alliance between two countries', and a 'common defense position'. This short-lived independence came to an end when some political parties and a section of the army rebelled against the king, to gain total freedom from British clutches. Britain retaliated by attacking Iraq and occupying it again, reinstalling the king and making Nuri as Said the Prime Minister, who was like a lapdog for the colonial powers.

The late 1940s and early 1950s signified the period when the wave of nationalism came forward in a stronger way. Nasser's nationalization of the Suez Canal had a very symbolic and strong message. The Soviet Union came to the support of some of these countries in their quest for nationalism. In 1958, a coup by a section of the military, led by Kasim, succeeded in throwing away the British puppets. Immediately, the United States and Britain threatened with military intervention. Finally, the United States extracted the promise of continuing its oil interests in the region as a tradeoff and the military attack was prevented. The new regime later demanded some respite from the grip of US and UK oil giants. They refused to budge. Kasim responded by withdrawing from the Baghdad Pact and struck a technical deal with the Soviet Union in 1959. To free Iraq from the stranglehold of IPC (Iraq Petroleum Corporation, controlled by the imperialists), Kasim floated a new oil company "...to develop the non-concessional lands, and revealed an American note threatening Iraq with sanctions unless he changed his position. He was overthrown in four days later in a coup that the Paris weekly *L'Express* stated flatly was 'inspired by the CIA'" (ibid., 27).

This coup was carried out by a section of the army in alliance with Ba'ath party (Arab Socialist Ba'ath party, Ba'ath renaissance). Ba'ath was soon thrown out and the rulers restored the concessions to the IPC. Anti-American and anti-British sentiments post 1976 war were very strong in the people's minds. The Iraqi government issued orders that the Iraq National Oil Company (INOC) alone would develop oil wells but the IPC would continue. The IPC during this period sabotaged the oil production to reduce the revenue coming to Iraq. The social and political turmoil started peaking toward disaster. In another coup, Ba'ath returned to power in 1968, with Saddam Hussein as the Vice President. Ba'ath made efforts to wriggle out of the control of the IPC with the help of the Soviet Union and France for technical help to develop the oil wells.

Iraq tried to wriggle away from imperialist control and develop social and economic projects within the country. Oil revenue helped a lot in this modernization. State welfare-ism was the key word. In contrast to the US allies in the area, Iraq developed very well. In addition to the US allies, Sheikhs were investing the revenues from oil in US banks, so indirectly the United States was benefiting from the rise in the oil prices, while Iraq invested it internally for its own development. Iraq was an eyesore for the Islamic fundamentalists as it opened up its social sphere for women. Education was the major agenda of the country.

The Iraq–Iran War

In 1979, Saddam Hussein became the President and Chairman of the Revolutionary Command Council. The overthrow of the Pahlavi dynasty, the puppet of the United States, came as a big blow to the US policies. Saddam succeeded in tapping the country's oil wealth for its own benefit and Iraq in turn became an ally of the USSR. It increased its military budget and became an important buyer of USSR arms. It had plans to go nuclear and emerge as the most powerful military regime in the area, next only to Israel. Border dispute became the cause of its war against Iran in 1980. This became a major opportunity for the United States to take advantage of the situation. Despite its ties with the USSR, Iraq turned to the West for support, which the United States and other Western countries were more than willing to offer. The diplomatic ties were revived with the United States and arms started being purchased. Iraq was using chemical weapons against Iran with full knowledge of the United States. Donald Rumsfeld, the architect of the 2002 aggression of Iraq, was the negotiator on behalf of the United States to arm Iraq. The United States also removed Iraq from the list of terrorist states and stopped UN from censuring Iraq for using chemical weapons in Iran.

> United States was the sole country to vote against a 1986 Security Council statement condemning Iraq's use of mustard gas against Iranian troops—an atrocity in which it now merges US was directly implicated.... US arranged massive loans for Iraq's burgeoning war expenditure from American client states such as Kuwait and Saudi Arabia. The US administration provided 'crop-spraying' helicopters (to be used for chemical attacks in 1998), let Dow Chemicals ship its chemicals for use on humans, seconded its air force officers to work with their Iraqi counterparts (from 1986) and approved technological exports to Iraq's missile procurement agency to extend the missiles' range (1988). (Research Unit for Political Economy, *Analytical Monthly Review*, May 2003, 31)

The US Defense Intelligence Agency prepared detailed battle plans for Iraqi forces in this period. The United States was keen that Iran be kept in check as its client states might feel threatened with the increase in the might of Iran. The United States did everything in its power to ensure that Iraq won over the strategic Fao Peninsula, which was a turning point in the battle and brought Iran to the negotiating table. A US senate inquiry revealed that during the Iran–Iraq war the United States had sent samples of all the strains of germs used by Iraq to make biological weapons. The United States fully backed Saddam in his suppression of the Kurds:

> As a part of Anfal campaign against the Kurds (Feb. to September 1988), the Iraqi regime used chemical weapons extensively against its own civilian population. Between 50,000 to 186,000 Kurds were killed in these attacks, over 1,200 Kurdish villages were destroyed and 300,000 Kurds were displaced.... The Anfal campaign was carried out with the acquiescence of the

west. Rather than condemn the massacre of Kurds, the US escalated its support to Iraq. It joined in Iraq's attacks on Iranian facilities, blowing up two Iranian oil rigs and destroying an Iranian frigate.... The US approved the export of items to Iraq of items of dual civilian and military use at double the rate in the aftermath of Halabja as it did before 1988. (Simpson and Ranwala 2002)

Attack on Iraq

Saddam had a very complex trajectory in Iraq. After coming to power, he did start the process of modernization of Iraq, and was fairly secular in his approach to social issues. He was not guided by clerics or by other so-called religious considerations. Iraq did begin its journey toward transformation in social relationships of gender and other feudal hierarchies. Modern education was given due importance and the plight of women in particular saw a rapid change toward equality. With the overthrow of the US stooge Reza Shah Pahlavi, and the coming in of the Islamic Revolution in Iran, under the leadership of Ayatollah Khomeini, the scene changed. Iraq was involved in an eight-year-long war, in which it was duly supported by the United States in the form of sharing of intelligence and supplying of arms in huge quantities. Saddam was looked up on as an ally by the Western powers, more so by the United States.

It was during this period that Islam began to be projected as a new threat to democracy by the United States, through its media and all other paraphernalia, consent for its policies in the popular mind and the global opinion against Islam began to be cultivated. It is during this period of alliance with the United States that the atrocities on Shias and Kurds were committed with impunity.

With Kuwait drawing out disproportionate oil through wells with a common source, Iraq became concerned and marched its armies on the Kuwaiti border. US ambassador Glisspe subtly hinted to Saddam that the United States had no opinion on the issue, meaning that he could do whatever he liked in the area. That was a good enough signal for Saddam to attack Kuwait and to declare it as its 24th state. The US turnaround came sooner than expected and it started shouting itself hoarse for protecting the sovereignty of Sheikhs of Kuwait. The attack on Iraq followed and sanctions were imposed on Iraq; the result was the killing of thousands of Iraqi people and crippling of infinite others, particularly children. When asked whether such an intense move was needed in Iraq, the US Secretary of State Madeleine Albright answered in the affirmative.

The United States designs in Iraq were to unfold gradually after its occupation of Afghanistan; the United States started saying that Iraq is in possession of WMD. The UN commissioners were deputed in Iraq who unequivocally gave the report that Iraq is not in possession of any such weapons. Undeterred by the UN report the United States went on to attack and occupy Iraq using its army. It was said that this army is the liberation army and will be welcomed with roses by the victims of Saddam. Soon imaginary roses turned into real guns and resistance movement picked up in Iraq. So far, while the US army has 'liberated', by killing, over five lakh Iraqis, the resistance reaction has sent over 5,000 body bags to the United States, the bags containing the bodies of the US soldiers on the 'mission democracy', the pet slogan of the United States in its design to control the world and appropriate the oil resources in the region.

In its blinded march for control over oil wells, the United States continued its project of demonizing Islam and creating Islamophobia, well supported by the elements with vested interests all over the world. Its policies in the oil-rich area have frightened a large section of the Muslim community all over the world, making it be perceived as the Great Satan. A large section of the Muslim community is wary of any step which is taken by the United States, the greatest violator of human rights in the world. There are other reasons for this also. The veneer of its democratic values is too thin and it keeps peeling off with every other move. Its shameless greed for oil and power is too obvious to be overlooked.

The United States has been, and is the biggest patron of the Sheikhs, tyrants, and dictators all over the world. Its claim that all this is being done to enhance democracy is totally bogus. Also, it violates the basic dictum that democracy cannot be imported from outside. The very notion of democracy rests on the will of the people, and free exercise of their mandate. With the US army breathing down the necks of people and committing the atrocities such as those being carried out in Abu Ghraib (naked human pyramids being made by the sadistic army to torture the Iraqis), one cannot think of any type of democracy, whatever the claims may be. Earlier, the USSR's project of 'exporting socialism' had met with a similar fate. These terms themselves are very contradictory in nature and betray more of the political goals of the exporter, rather than the popular ambitions of the people at the grassroots level where they are imposed. The United States has taken this game a bit too far, and with the decline of the other pole of power, the USSR, its aggressive stance is a step ahead of the earlier imperial powers, the ones that colonized a large part of the globe in pursuit of markets and raw material.

Another interesting part of the story is how uniformly the colonizers, imperial powers, pursue the divide and rule policy. For their own self, they project a secular identity, and for their ruled subjects, they use the religious, sectarian identity. That is what the British did to prop up Muslim communalism (the Muslim League) and Hindu communalism (Hindu Mahasabha, RSS) in India. They themselves never identified themselves as Christian rulers. In Iraq, the Shia–Sunni identity has intensified after the US occupation of Iraq, and now after Saddam's execution it will worsen further. In democratic societies, over a period of time, narrow sectarian identities get secondary status to overarching secular identities. Under the rule of external powers, whatever be their slogan, sectarian identities grow and dominate the social and political scene.

While one condemns Saddam for his dictatorial methods and atrocities against Shias and Kurds, one realizes that he also emerged as a symbol of resistance against the imperialist acts of the United States. Starting from the US invasion of Iraq in 1990, to the occupation of Afghanistan and later Iraq, the insecurity amongst a section of the Muslim masses is hitting the roof. In such a situation, if a tyrant like Saddam defies US dictates, he naturally emerges as a hero. It has more to do with the targeting of Muslims than with the 'virtues' of the ilk of Saddam Hussein. It is defiance against the oppressor that gives hope to the demonized and oppressed sections; it cannot be construed as the sanction for the tyranny committed by them. Surely today the United States is the bully-in-chief, and so every powerful voice against it sounds as a voice of hope for millions.

There is another analogy that comes to one's mind. When the British ruled India, they also partitioned the country. The US policies have already aggravated the sectarian divides between the Shias, Sunnis, and Kurds. The imminent aggravation of civic strife is on the cards. The US policies are to be blamed for this.

As a sidelight, in Indian scenario, the RSS has been the permanent defender of the US attacks and aggressions around the world. Starting from the US butchery in Vietnam to the current US polices in Iraq, RSS has supported the US Invasions. At the time of attack on Iraq by the US armies, the RSS chief vociferously defended the US aggression. In this case, there may be malice in the heart of this organization in treating Muslims as their 'permanent enemies' and attacking them one way or the other. And this may be one of the reasons for the BJP to look the other way when Saddam boldly faced the gallows. So martyr for some and villain for the other!

The hanging of Saddam, though sudden, was expected. Since the time he was captured by the US armies and a case put up against him by the Iraqi government, it was evident that Saddam was dangerous to the United States as long as he was alive. He has been done away with through mock justice, 'judicial assassination' as someone has put it, or through the justice of the Kangaroo court set up by the occupation army, under the guise of a democratically elected government.

The reaction to this has been extremely diverse. President Bush has hailed it as a path to democracy in Iraq. Of course, democracy is projected to be the major plank of the US policy, but in fact it is just a slogan for the US invasions around the world. A section of the Kurds and Shias have celebrated the event with joy as Saddam had been oppressive against both Kurds and Shias during his dictatorial regime. In India, the Congress has come out to criticize the hanging, while RSS progeny BJP has preferred to stay quiet on the issue. A large section of observers have displayed their dismay over the way things are shaping up in West Asia, while the Arab world has condemned this act. A large section of the Muslim community has been deeply upset over this and has shown intense displeasure over the hanging.

Pakistan

Pakistan came into being due to the British policy of divide and rule and complex political movements of the landlords and their affiliates in India. The Muslim League was formed in Dhaka in 1906 and Hindu Mahasabha succeeded Punjab Hindu Sabha formed in the early 20th century (1915). The Muslim League claimed that it was formed to look after the interests of Muslims, but it never took up any issues of poor Muslims and restricted itself to the demands of the elite sections of Muslims. The failure of reconciliation between the major communal parties and Congress led to the Muslim League demanding Pakistan, and the British, bent upon partitioning the country, came in handy in the process of the formation of Pakistan. The landlords were joined by sections of educated Muslims and elite Muslims in the demand for Pakistan. The average Muslim in this country was aloof from this demand. Muhammad Ali Jinnah, who began his career as a secular Congress leader, dissociated himself from the mass movements launched by the Congress under the leadership of Mahatma Gandhi and later went on to become the leader of the Muslim League. Muslims in India were not a homogeneous community. Also, the geographical and ethnic differences were very deep. That is how most of the Muslims of India rallied to the secular democratic movement of the Congress than to the Muslim League.

The Pakistan Muslim League used Islam as a symbol for political integration of the country.

> No Muslim league leader ever invoked 'Islamic Ideology' during the independence movement. Nor was Muslim league able to generate an Islamic National consciousness among the Muslim of India, least of all in the Muslim majority area which later became Pakistan, despite all the pep-talk of Pakistan. (Gardezi 2001, 35)

Pakistan was mainly the demand of a party that was

> dominated by Jagirdars of north India, an area which was the cradle of Muslim power. The merchants of western India were at best, junior partners in the power structure of Muslim League, and of course, there were no industrial bourgeois families among Muslims worth the name, which could influence its policies. After partition Pakistan was ruled by an alliance of landlords, bureaucrats and military. (Engineer 1994, 151)

It was logical that after the demise of Muhammad Ali Jinnah, the feudal elements would take over and abolish whatever little possibility of democracy there was in Pakistan. The Muslim League was not a party with mass character.

> Pakistan was largely agricultural country at the time of partition, and inherited from the British a feudal, colonial economy...a large proportion of

population lived on the land, where agriculture was dominated by feudal property relations. Peasants who were exploited by cruel and tyrannical landlords tilled the land in a most primitive manner. Six thousand landlords in West Pakistan owned more land than the 3.3 million peasant householders. (Ali 1970, 37)

The type of industrialization which developed in Pakistan was very peculiar, "a capitalism of colonial type, backward, predominantly agrarians, heavily tinged with practices inherited from the feudal past" (Rodinson 1974, 131). Due to the prevalence of feudal structures, the benefits of social facilities remained restricted to a handful, the majority remaining untouched by social progress. Lack of industrialization and lack of modernization generally go together.

The idea of Pakistan as an Islamic state started emerging soon after independence. Islamic parties started to use religion in political arena and mullahs began to orchestrate the need for Islamic rule in the country; they started talking about 'Islamic ideology', 'Islamic nationhood', etc. Jinnah, who at the core was a democrat, saw the danger signals and warned, "You may belong to any religion, caste or creed—that has nothing to do with the business of state." With Jinnah's death a year later, the orthodox parties and mullahs had no significant opposition to the march of fundamentalism. "The Pakistani state became an arena in which various contenders of power—the Muslim League leaders of different class and ethnic backgrounds, the powerful civil servants and generals, the religious maulanas—began to vie with each other for hegemony" (Gardezi 2001, 35). The series of coups d'état, and one military dictator replacing the other, were followed by brief interludes of democracy, and Islam was used to legitimize the changes in regime. The seeds of this were sown by the Objectives Resolution moved in the Constituent Assembly. The resolution declared that

> [S]overeignty in Pakistan rests with God Almighty and also affirmed the role of state in enabling Muslims to order their lives in accord with teachings of Islam…the same assembly stipulating that head of the state shall be a Muslim and a board of five ulema would check that no legislation contravened the injunctions of Holy Koran and Sunna, the prophetic tradition. (ibid., 36)

The Constituent Assembly had mandated that the country's first ever general elections would be held in March 1959. This never happened as to preempt the democracy, the army, under instructions from the bureaucracy and the United States, seized power in October 1958, initiating the triangle of power centers in the Pakistan army, the mullahs, and the United States. This threw light on both the aspects of the international politics, the liberal West's dislike for democracy in the countries coming out from the clutches, and the nexus of the army, the mullahs, and the United States. The 1956 Constitution gave Pakistan the name of Islamic Republic; in 1962, General Ayub replaced the ulema by the Advisory Council; and in 1973, Bhutto proclaimed Islam as the state religion. Needless to say, the state of Pakistan was backed by the US imperialists in their strategic game in South Siam, as a counter to the Soviet Union and the non-aligned Indian State.

Zia-ul-Haq did away with all pretenses and derived the legitimacy of his rule directly from Allah. He lived the adage that sharia flourishes under the shadow of the sword. His ordinances were against the interests of women, workers, and minorities.

Pakistan was always pro-West, and the United States had deep roots in the administration of Pakistan. It toed the US policies on a global scale. In the case of the Suez crisis, when Washington withdrew its initial offer of support for reconstruction, it was pointed out that its loyal ally Pakistan opposed this move of the United States, "New York Times claimed that loyal allies Pakistan, Iran and Turkey had argued vociferously against the 'biggest single US aid project' being granted to a country that was 'not only neutral but occasionally anti-Western'" (Ali 2003, 104).

The East Pakistan (EP) assembly was against the tie-up with the United States, but it was overruled by the administration, which was dominated by West Pakistan (WP). The internal problems between WP and EP were also simmering as WP was exploiting EP and the military and the occasional democratic face opposed the aspirations of EP. The speech of one Bengali (EP) leader in the assembly was reflective of the interrelation between the two parts of Pakistan.

> Sir, I actually started yesterday and said that the attitude of the Muslim League coteries here was of contempt towards E Bengal, towards it culture,

its language, its literature and everything concerning EB.... In fact, Sir, I tell you that far from considering the EB as equal partner, the leaders of the Muslim League thought we were a subject race and that they belonged to a race of conquerors.

The tragic events of 26/11, the Mumbai terror attack, have brought forward different responses from diverse sections of society. The most common one is that since the terror groups are based in Pakistan, the attack should be launched on Pakistan to wipe out the training centers located there. The popular yoga guru Baba Ramdev with massive following expressed that this is the right time to teach Pakistan a lesson.

Pakistan President Asif Ali Zardari, in an article in the New York Times, argues that the terror training camps located in Pakistan were propped up and supported by the United States to train the terrorists to fight against the Soviet occupation of Afghanistan during the Cold War era. It is clear that these bases and the indoctrinated terrorists, who are a product of these camps, have been brainwashed into perpetrating violence on the misplaced notions of kafir, enemy; this concept of kafir was instilled in the minds of the youth in these US-supported madrassas.

Will attacking Pakistan help matters? Frankenstein's monsters created for the pursuance of political goals are easy to produce and difficult to control and eradicate once their political utility is over. Khalistanis were similarly promoted to go more and more into extremism; Sikhism was invoked as a cloak for this politics. Later, the same monsters turned against the forces which aided in their creation. Not surprisingly, Al Qaeda clones later turned their guns against their creators and others.

With Zardari stating the truth about the US designs in floating Al Qaeda, and the researchers working in the area reaffirming this, the truth of this phenomenon has been reinforced. The truth is that US imperialism is capable of creating monsters for its political goals and then these elements continue to cause havoc later on. The biggest harm caused by the United States couching its political–economic ambitions in religious language has been the demonization of a religion and a religious community with tragic consequences for the community.

Reaching the truth is like reaching the transparent water in a coconut. Many social understandings stop short of the transparent water and identify the coconut with its outer layers alone. So much paper has been blackened likening terrorism with Islam and Muslims. The average common sense stopped short of the truth of the US involvement in the whole game. Our social common sense is reflected by what a saffron-robed swami has said.

The state of Pakistan as such has been a victim of the colonial power design in the pre-Independence era, and later, it has been mauled and used by the United States for maintaining its hegemony in the oil-rich zone. Most political commentators will equate the formation of Pakistan with Muslim separatism. The fact is that the British policy of divide and rule encouraged the Muslim and Hindu elites to put forth a two-nation theory, which was initially theorized by V.D. Savarkar. A handful of elite were behind the idea of separate Muslim and Hindu nations, but the British gave them importance out of proportion to their social base. The politics of hate propagated by these communal formations intensi-fied the communal violence, resulting in severe cracks in the concept of composite Indian nationalism, which further led to the partition of the country. More than the Muslim League, it was the British design of having a long-term control in the region that resulted in the formation of Pakistan. Hindu communalists have to share equal blame as they also said that nationalism is based on religion, that there are two nations within the country, and that Muslims would have to be subordinate to the Hindu nation.

The US empire substituted the declining British Empire-turned Pakistan into a semi-vassal state, using it as its military base, to control the whole oil zone. In Pakistan, the US hegemony is as much responsible for stifling the democratic process as the hold of mullahs and the army. We have to recognize that today a very positive process of development of democracy is going on in Pakistan. The elements which will benefit by attacking Pakistan will be those opposed to democracy, the mullahs, and the army. The United States seems to have milked Pakistan as much as it needed and now is looking for shifting its base to South Asia.

Attacking Pakistan at this point is what the fanatic elements in Pakistan and India want. The response to 26/11 has been cleverly modulated into becoming anti-Pakistan hysteria. The demand for attack on Pakistan will well serve both the fanatics in Pakistan and the fanatics in India. Their interests match most of the times. It is sheer insanity to think of attacking a country armed with nuclear weapons, and it also means strengthening the arms of the Pakistan army and mullahs.

A joint endeavor by both the democratic governments is needed to honestly investigate the Mumbai terror attacks, and to punish the guilty. If possible, India should take steps which strengthen the Pakistani government in its own battle against the army and mullahs. This strengthening of the democratic process will help India as much as Pakistan, if not more. One can see the change in the language of the Pakistani government since the military is cooling its heels in the barracks and the democratic process has taken over the centers of power. One hopes that the Indian government does not fall into the trap laid by Pakistani fundamentalists and is able to overcome the exhortation hysteria of sections calling for the blood of Pakistan in an act of blind revenge, while ensuring that terror acts are controlled.

The Death of Osama bin Laden and the Changing World

The declaration of the death of Osama bin Laden (May 2, 2011) is mired with many mysteries. It is also full of blatant violations of the international law (http://www.nbcnews.com/id/42852700/ns/world_news-death_of_bin_laden/t/us-forces-kill-osama-bin-laden-pakistan/ [last accessed on September 1, 2014]). It does have a profound impact on the future of global politics. Osama and Al Qaeda had been dominating the global political scenario overtly for the past decade or so, and covertly through their activities for the past two–three decades. West Asia–Indian subcontinent have been the major victim of their dreaded acts; still, the death of this Frankenstein's monster has been accompanied by infinite questions and implications.

To begin with, there had been various news items claiming that Osama is dead, time and time again. Pakistan's ex-Prime Minister Benazir Bhutto, who herself became a victim of terrorism, had declared Osama bin Laden is already dead. Anyway, what matters is the popular perceptions and the 'understanding'. This understanding, 'manufactured or real', is propagated by the global emperor, the United States, and the dominating US media. This seems to be more important than the truth. Truth shall ultimately prevail, but in the short run, the propaganda and perceptions do dictate the global and local scenarios. So, in that sense now, Osama is really dead for good.

The manner of his killing reminds us as to who is the biggest violator of international law—a superpower, with its tentacles spread all over the world, itching to undertake actions in the name of democracy and peace, but in reality protecting its interests of controlling oil wealth and maintaining global supremacy, the United States. Its armed forces blatantly violated Pakistan's airspace, ignored its sovereignty, and killed an unarmed Osama. Noam Chomsky, the indefatigable human rights conscience keeper, poses an interesting question: What if the Pakistani army or some other army lands up in army White House, kills someone there, and dumps his body in the sea? Unthinkable, no?

Osama could have been captured and tried in the international court of law and punished accordingly. Why did an unarmed man, a criminal, have to be killed is beyond imagination in the civil world with so many laws and norms. It seems laws and conventions are for the ordinary mortals and states; for some States (the United States) the medieval 'might is right' and 'we are the law' still prevail. This is a warning signal for the whole of humanity, reminding us of the need for reviving international bodies like the UN not just formally but de facto, with real flesh and blood. Organizations like the UN not only need to be revived and democratized, they also have to be endowed with legal and moral authority to mediate in international affairs. The arbitrary 'cowboy' norms need to be condemned and done away with.

This 'death of Osama' should open a new chapter in global and local politics (http://www.wanttoknow.info/020318chicagotribune [last accessed on October 10, 2014]). The previous decade has been dictated by the US policy of oil hunt by creating the theory of 'clash of civilizations' (http://www.foreignaffairs.com/articles/48950/samuel-p-huntington/the-clash-of-civilizations [last accessed on October 10, 2014]), a theory which is an insult to the humane values of mankind, a concept which deliberately overlooks the deeper alliance of people and civilizations. This clash of civilizations theory implemented by the United States projected Islam as a threat to democracy and freedom, irrespective of the fact that the United States itself is the same global power which overthrew democracies and promoted dictatorships in the area for its economic political agenda. The overthrow of the democratically elected Mossadeq regime in Iran (1953) had set the scene for the imposition of authoritarian regimes in this area. Again, the processes that have begun in Tunisia, Egypt, etc. are reminders that Arab Muslims aspire for democracy as much as any other people in the world and are trying to overthrow the yoke of dictatorial regimes.

The US invasions on different countries in the region were justified by the 'global supercop' by projecting Islam and Muslims as being backward, which projected the myth that it is playing the role of savior. With the death of Osama bin Laden, this chapter of dark global politics should be over, and the region should be left to its own moral and political resources to develop political systems, away from the interference of outsiders. Democracy is basically a grassroots process. It cannot be 'exported' or 'imposed' on others. The efforts should be to let local alliances emerge, to let global democracy amongst nations emerge, and let the local population decide their path for achieving a democratic system. It is on these issues that all the concerned peace movements assert the values of peace and democracy through mass demonstrations. These voices and peace campaigns should act as a brake to the hegemonic policies of the superpower.

As far as India and Pakistan are concerned, the whole talk of repeating Abbottabad by a particular section in India needs to be rejected outright. The Indian political leadership has shown political maturity and offered the dialogue table for achieving friendship with the neighbor. The same should be enhanced. On the one hand, we need to firmly deal with criminal elements, by promoting trust and amity between nations, and on the other, cooperation in the area of culture, trade, commerce, and education needs to be boosted. We need to not only be restricted to Pakistan, but also revive the spirit of the South Asian Association for Regional Cooperation (SAARC) at a deeper and broader level.

Some claim that the May 2011 death of Osama is the ninth time he is being declared dead; but it is a boon to the process of peace anyway. The demonization of Islam and Muslims will hopefully end. Morality of all religions has been a great contribution to the development of the human values of mankind. All religious communities have contributed to the progress of the human race, and this needs to be the major slogan in the coming decades.

3
Islam:
Through the Ages

Islam, which today is regarded as the fountainhead of violence, actually means submission. The word 'Islam' is etymologically related to salaam, meaning peace. It began in the year 632 and was founded by Prophet Muhammad. It is one of the three major world religions, and number-wise it is the second largest religion in the world. It came into being in western Arabia in the beginning of the seventh century when the patriarchal–communal social order was breaking down and class-based Arab states were coming into being. At that time, Arabs were in an extremely backward state and were divided into small warring tribes. "They were fighting with each other and plundering each other. There was no social or political order, no rules or regulation to go by. Idol worship was rampant and each tribe had their own idols. These ranged in thousands" (Sharma 2003, 65).

Arabia was populated by Semitic tribes who are the ancestors of today's Arabs.

> Some of them were settled in oases and cities, engaged in farming, craft and trade; some were nomads in the plains and deserts, breeding camels, horses, sheep and goats. Arabia was economically and culturally connected with neighboring countries—Mesopotamia, Syria, Palestine, Egypt and Ethiopia. The trade routes between these countries went through Arabia. One of the important crossroads was in Meccan oasis, near the coast of Red Sea. The tribal nobility of Koreish people profited a great deal from this trade. (Tokarey 1986, 308)

Mecca started becoming more and more important. "The city of Mecca had grown into an important center of international trade. Merchants from different nations gathered at Mecca to launch new enterprises" (Engineer 1987, 39). The religious center of all Arabs developed in Mecca over a period of time. With the change in the trade route in the sixth century, caravan trade began to decline. Nomads lost their income and started taking to farming. With this, the need for land grew and clashes began amongst tribes. The tribal humanism was prevalent in the pre-Islamic period, but it was

> incapable of theorizing its practice or using it to unite the tribes, let alone raising it the level of universal philosophy of existence. One reason of this was profusion of gods and goddesses. These were nothing but the superhuman version of the human, but belief in them perpetuated tribal divisions and disputes, often caused by commercial rivalries. (Ali 2003, 28)

With the collapse of old tribal values of taking care of the weak, the Quresh tribes were more intent on making money at the expense of the poor of the tribe.

> There was spiritual restlessness in Mecca throughout the Peninsula. Arabs knew that Judaism and Christianity, which were practiced in Byzantine and Persian empires, were more sophisticated than their own pagan traditions. Some had come to believe that high God of their pantheon, Al-Lah (whose name simply means God) was a deity worshipped by Jews and Christians, but he had sent the Arabs no prophet and no scripture of in their own language. (Armstrong 2002, 3)

In this background, Muhammad expressed the values which were to unify communities and later to lay the foundation of a religious community, and the social powers which were to use the identity of this religion for their kingdoms.

> Mohammad's spiritual drive was partially fuelled by socio-economic passions, by the desire to strengthen the commercial standing of Arabs and the need to impose a set of common rules. His vision encompassed a tribal confederation unite by the common goals and loyal to a single faith which, of necessity, must be both new and universal. Islam became the cement utilized by Mohammad to unite Arab tribes and from the beginning, it regarded commerce as the only noble occupation. (Ali 2003, 29)

These ideas did make a significant change in the way communities were living and interacting,

> Ideas, especially religious ideas have an important part to play in the adjustment of a social system to a change in the material environment...the immediate result of the material change is the social maladjustment, and this involves dissatisfaction and discontent in the members of the society.... They do not become effective movements until they have a positively conceived goals, and this if it is to be consciously accepted by many members of the society, must be expressed in ideas. (Montgomery Watt Mohammad, London, 45–46, quoted in Engineer 1987, 47)

The main point in understanding the origin of Islam is the nature of Meccan society at that time. "In the absence of state machinery the only way of maintaining law and order in the society was to depend on the cooperation of tribes to enforce the mala's unanimous decisions" (Engineer 1987, 47). Islam as an emerging faith had to address the tensions created as a result of the breakup of tribal morality, by going back to tribal collectivism, as that would have shattered the commercial structure and created newer tensions which have been more difficult to answer. Muhammad's ingenuity comes into play at this particular point; he

> upheld the new progressive change in the society while, to remove the tensions caused by the new change, he picked those values of tribal society, which without coming in to conflict with the historical change struck a balance between individualism and collectivism. Thus in Meccansuras, which are terse and forceful he exhorts the Meccan rich to take care of the poor, the indigent and needy orphans and widows. (Engineer 1987, 50)

The teachings of Muhammad are a response to the widening gulf between the rich and poor in Arabian society.

> Thus it can be inferred that Mohammad owing to gross inequalities between rich and poor and the widening gap between them, had realized that if nothing was done to contain the danger the society would soon be broken in to pieces, smashed up by the wrath of people, which spread like wild fire. (Engineer 1987, 56)

Muhammad was born on April 22, 570 CE, in the clan of the merchant's tribe of Queresh of Mecca, which was a trading post in western Arabia and was also a place of pilgrimage for worshippers of idols at the sanctuary of Kaaba, a small square temple containing the sacred black stone, which was probably a fallen meteorite. Muhammad was a quiet man, serious and reflective. The teachings of Islam are compiled in the Quran, which comprises of 114 *suras* (chapters), and 6,616 verses. Quran means recitation or discourse. From 613, Muhammed began preaching the divine revelations to small groups of relatives and friends. His message in brief was: "Abandon all forms of idolatrous worship and surrender yourself completely to omniscient and omnipotent, yet compassionate Allah. He warned the wealthy that considering that accumulation of riches as an end in itself and being niggardly would lead them to catastrophe" (Hiro 1988, 6).

He started getting converts to his teachings. Many of these were poor and women who also started to accept the new faith, and many were those who were disturbed by the new inequity the society. His teachings were basically simple. He pointed out that it was wrong to build private fortune, but good to share wealth and create a society where , and weak and poor are treated with respect. "The new sect would eventually be called Islam (surrender); a Muslim was a man or a woman who had made this submission of their entire being to Allah and his demand that human beings behave with one another with justice, equity and compassion" (Armstrong 2002, 5). *Zakat* (compulsory alms-giving) was very important so that the poor and destitute could be taken care of by the society. The Ramadan, fasting for a whole month, was meant to be a reminder of the privations of the poor. "Social justice was, therefore, the crucial virtue of Islam. Muslims were commanded as their first duty to build a community (Ummah) characterized by practical compassion, in which there was a fair distribution of wealth" (ibid., 6). The Quran insists that its message is simply a reminder of the truths already known to sections of humanity. God has sent messengers to every part of the world. "Constantly the Quran points out that Muhammad had not come to cancel older religions, to contradict their prophets or to start a new faith. His message is the same as that of Abraham, Moses, David, Solomon or Jesus" (ibid., 7). Most scholars of Islam point out that had Muhammad or the Arab world known about the prophets from India, or Australia, those also would have been recognized as messengers of Allah. The Quran does mention that there shall be no coercion in the matters of religion. It also commands its followers to respect the people of other religions.

Islamic worship is based on five pillars of faith: There is no God but Allah, and Muhammad is the apostle of God; performance of divine worship five times a day; fasting during the month of Ramadan; compulsory alms giving (zakat); and pilgrimage to Mecca (hajj) if at all possible. The future changes in Islam got reflected in Sunna—the body of traditional Islamic law based on words and deeds of Muhammad, recounted in the series of legends or Hadith.

His monotheistic teachings angered the rich of Mecca, as they were the beneficiaries of the pilgrims coming to worship different idols. By demanding allegiance to one God, Muhammad created a loyalty, which went beyond traditional allegiance to the clan, and this was the reason for the powerful clan leaders getting upset with Muhammad. In 620, during their visit to Kaaba, some members of the Khazarah tribal federation from the oasis of Yathrib, known as Medina, embraced Islam. Muhammad left Mecca in 622; this is called Hegira, the beginning of the Muslim, as it was from here that Islamic values were fully applied in the society. Before this, tribe was the most important identity and association. Now, Muhammad came to be head of a community comprising diverse tribes, something that was unheard of earlier. In Medina, he got a larger following, and later united the greater part of Arabia around Islam. In Medina, the feuding tribes of Aus and Khazraj welcomed Muhammad as an arbitrator, and later they also accepted Islam. The Madina section of the Quran focuses more on the current affairs and provides a corpus of law. In addition to other norms, family norms are given advice about. Women are given the right to own and inherit property; they are awarded the same rights in marriage and divorce as men. The duties of men are outlined and provision of having four wives is there with many conditions (if you fear you will not be equitable [to them] then only [one]). The permission for polygamy was context-specific as men were being killed in the internecine battles raging at that time. The Koran lays down the norms of human behavior, decency relating to theft, crime, adultery, etc.

It is in Medina that Muhammad laid the foundation of Islamic Ummah and Dar al-Islam, realm of Islam. The People with backgrounds of diverse faiths had to be brought together as a single community.

If they did not hold together Islam could not become an effective force in Median. It might not even survive! Yet in Muhammad's mind there were more than merely pragmatic reasons for striving to create a unified community. At stake was an important principle—the principle that a new solidarity was being born that transcended all the previous loyalties. The oneness of God must be translated into oneness of believers. (Miller 2000, 106)

The formation of Muslim Ummah did result in wars when needed, and following a series of victories, Muhammad entered Mecca in 630. The polytheistic tribes started taking to Islam in large numbers. In accordance with the need of the time, all the activities were made part of the mosque, no separation between mundane and sacred and political and religious was made. Islam was the major religion to give rights to women, rights of inheritance and divorce. "The Koran prescribes some degree of segregation and veiling for prophets wives, but there is nothing in Koran that requires veiling of all women or their segregation in separate part of the house" (Armstrong 2002, 14).

In 630–631, under Muhammad's leadership, the Muslims gained control of Mecca and later large parts of Arabia, where Islam took root. The tribal aristocracy did put up a resistance to the spread of Islam. Despite that, it spread rapidly due to the simplicity of its teachings; it also showed the Bedouins the way to survive by getting more land, which was a major problem in that community.

Even during the time when the Prophet was alive, tussle started about who would succeed him, and this came out in the open after his death. Muhammad had already declared himself as the last prophet. After his death, the tradition of *Khilafat* (caliphate) started. Abu Bakr, father of Muhammad's wife Ayesha, became the first *Khalifa* (chief ruler). *Khalifa* Omar, *Khalifa* Usma, and then Ali succeeded him. This issue of succession also started taking the ideological veneer, leading to the rise of many sects in Islam. The initial division was between Shias and Sunnis. The followers of Ali came to be known as Shias and the followers of Abu came to be known as Sunnis. Their main difference began around the issue of *Khilafat*. Shias regard Ali as the first *Khalifa*, and according to them the first three *Khalifas* had assumed that power by fraud. They regard descendants of Ali as the *Khalifa*. Later, many other sects were to come up over a period of time—Abbasi, Ummaid, Kuriash Kadiani, Sufi, Ahmadi,Wahabi, etc.

Muhammad's successors captured the neighboring and then remote countries, in the Mediterranean and east. Caliphs Abu Bakr, Omar, and Osma conquered neighboring and then more remote areas in a brief period of time. These conquests were carried out under the banner of Islam.

> There was nothing religious about these campaigns, and Umar did not believe that he had a divine mandate to conquer the world. The objective of Umar and his warriors was entirely pragmatic; they wanted plunder and a common activity that would preserve the unity of Ummah. For centuries Arabs had tried to raid the richer settled lands beyond the peninsula. The difference was that this time they had encountered a power vacuum. Persia and Byzantine had both been engaged for decades in long and debilitating series of wars with one another. Both were exhausted. (Armstrong 2002, 25)

It is later that religious interpretation was given to these wars.

The factor aiding their victories related to the inner dynamics of the empires, which were won over, as they were riddled with inner contradictions. The Byzantine and Sassanid Empires were terribly oppressed by the feudal lords, and there was no resistance to the march of Arabs.

> The fervor of unified Arab tribes cannot be explained simply by the appeal of new religion or promise or pleasure of paradise. It was the comforts of this world that motivated the tens of thousands who flocked to fight under the command of Khalid ibn-Walid and took part in the conquest of Damascus. The ninth century weaver poet Abu Tammam referred this in a verse
> No, not for the Paradise didst thou the nomad life forsake:
> Rather, I believe, it was thy yearning after bread and dates. (Ali 2003, 32)

In the countries won over, the obligations, taxes on the population were reduced, more so if they embraced Islam. This helped in the spread of Islam, and Islam soon turned into a world religion. By the eighth century, Islam became the major and only religion of these areas, spread from Spain to Central Asia to the borders of India. Between the 11th and the 18th century, it spread to different parts of India. It also spread to Indonesia between the 14th and the 16th century through Arab and Indian merchants and supplemented the Buddhism and Hinduism.

Over a period of time, the contradictions in the society led to the rise of different sects within Islam. These sects represented different ethnic, class, and national interests. While the Shiite movement is seen as the struggle for power between the followers of one or the other *Khalifa*, it was an expression of national sentiments of Persians against the Arabs who conquered them. It was the struggle of peasants and feudal lords against the Arab conquerors. The death of Ali was followed by the spread of Shiism in Iran and Iraq as an expression of protest against the power of the Arab caliphate. "According to Shiite legend, Ali and his sons Hasan and Hessian died as martyrs to the faith" (Tokarey 1986, 375). Shiites believe that *Khalifa* can come only from the descendants of Muhammad; they reject Sunna, which was compiled by the first caliph out of legends of the prophet. In due course of time, different trends emerged. The major Shia tradition recognizes 11 legitimate imams, the descendants of Ali. It holds the belief that during the ninth century, the 12th imam hid himself and still exists somewhere invisible waiting for the time when he will appear as the savior (*Mahdi*). This trend became very strong in Iran to the extent of Islam becoming the official religion there in 16th century.

Of the other smaller Shia sects in the eighth century, Ismail founded one, which goes in his name; this is popular in the mountain regions of Afghanistan and also in parts of India. For them, the world spirit is embodied in their imams. These imams form a hereditary dynasty, the Aga Khans, who collect tribute from their followers. Similarly, Bohras is another Islamic sect, which also collects huge tributes from its followers. Carmathians and Druses are some other sects coming from this stream.

Sunnism is the major sect of orthodox Islam, which is practiced by most Muslims in the world. They do recognize the Sunnas. It has further subsects. In the eighth and ninth centuries, Mu'tazilites came into being. They tried to understand Islamic doctrines in a rational way and maintained that God is just that, man has free will, that Koran is a book written by people and not created by God. Some Caliphs did support this trend to support their weakening hold on the community. But later, orthodox clergy started persecuting them.

In Muslim theology, four schools of thought developed in the eighth and ninth centuries: Hanifite, Shafiite, Malikite, and Hanbalite. These were named after their founders. The Hanbalite School was extremely fanatic and stuck to the literal translation of religious dogmas. It became the strongest amongst the backward Bedouin population in Arabia.

The Malikite School became prominent in North Africa. The other two streams were more open to the liberal interpretation of Islam.

Sufism is an important stream in different parts of the world it became rooted in India between 8th and 10th centuries. The word 'Sufi' means coarse wool fabric, the type of clothes worn by Sufi mystics. It grew within Shiism, but over time, some Sunnis also took to this sect. It was influenced by the ideas of Mazdaism, perhaps Buddhism and neo-Platonism. It has strong streaks of mysticism. To begin with, it gave no importance to rituals and tried to have true understanding of God. It tried to transcend the anthropomorphic understanding of Allah, looking at him more as a spiritual authority. Many Sufi, had pantheistic beliefs and they articulated their values in a very humane way. They believed in the omnipresence of God and looked at the world as a manifestation of the being of Allah. In the beginning, the orthodox sects started persecuting them, but later compromises were struck. The Sufis formed the orders of roving monks, dervishes. People of all religions in many countries frequent their shrines. Many dervishes employ dance and song as the major practice of their faith. Many deviations plagued different Sufi sects.

The Wahabi movement developed in modern times. It was more popular amongst nomads and the poor. They did not recognize the trends of saints and emphasized on worship of God alone; they also advocated for return to the patriarchal simplicity of early Islamic society. Many a contemporary phenomenon found expression in the Islamic sects. In the middle of the 19th century in Persia, the discontent of urban poor and peasants took the form of the Babite movement. Bab, its founder, declared himself as the successor of Muhammad and taught equality and brotherhood amongst all those who were Muslims. Similarly, the Mahdi movement came up in Sudan in 1881 against colonialism. Its leader Muhammad Ahmad declared himself as Mahdi (savior, messiah) and led the struggle against colonizers.

Islam as such does not distinguish between the secular and profane divisions. Islam guides all personal, family, social, and political matters. As per Qamaruddin Khan, Professor of Islamic History, Karachi University, "Quran does not aim to create a state but to create a society" (Khan 1983, 4). As such, Islam has no priestly principle; it has a strong principle of equality of all believers.

There is no one that can stand between the individual believer and God. There is no one endowed with special authority or responsibility to mediate God's graces to humanity. To use example of other religion, there is no pope, church council, voting convention or ordination ceremony for clergy. Clergy does not have powers that laity do not have. (Miller 2000, 147)

Overall, the clergy developed in Islam like in any other religion. The need for someone to lead the prayer, preach sermons, and interpret Islam led to the rise of the clergy. In kingdoms, a section of the clergy allied with the rulers and played the role akin to that of the church and the pope in medieval times. Different aspects of the Muslim clergy emerged, despite the fact that the clergy as such does not have a sanctioned place in Islam. A mullah is a teacher in a mosque, a *qadi* is a judge who specializes in sharia, mufti is the main authority of sharia, and ulema a learned theologian and teacher in a religious school. Muslim clergy in practice is headed by a *Sheikh ul-Islam*, a prominent theologian who is the rules adviser.

Spread of Islam

Beginning from Arabia, Islam gradually spread far and wide, encompassing many territories and populations. Many political, social, and spiritual factors helped in this spread. The simplicity of Islamic teachings, the religious zeal of its followers, the concept of *jihad* being interpreted as expanding the Islamic mandate beyond the existing borders, and strong leadership of the Muslim forces were the primary causes of its expansion. The major incentive for the Arabs to cross their boundaries was the expectation of booty accruing from winning over new lands. Assisting this expectation to surge further was the power vacuum left behind by struggle between the Eastern Roman Empire, Byzantium, and Persia. Their perennial battles leading to their exhaustion were probably the primary reason for the advance of Arab forces. Christian powers by this time were divided ethnically and theologically, and the power struggles and controversies, which acted as cover for that, were too numerous.

Peaceful preaching of the religion followed as the Muslim kings advanced territorially by military conquests, and these conquests led to the spread of Islam. The military conquests were motivated by the profane goals of power and pelf. The areas won over by war were the ones where the population comprised of Christians, Jews, and Zoroastrians. The Koran has recognized them as 'people of the book' and accorded them special status.

It was also not in the best interests of conquerors to pressure or compel the conversion of these populations, for the large non-Muslim groups provided a strong tax base for the conquerors. There were some zealous Muslims who violated the policy, especially when rebellions occurred, but on the whole the principle was maintained. (Miller 2000, 333)

The other method of Muslim numerical expansion was emigration, immigration, trading contacts, and intermarriage. Various Muslim empires came up over a period of time. The Umayyad Dynasty (680–750) was centered around Damascus in Syria, non-Arab-oriented, monarchical, and secular in its policies. Its imperial style had nothing to do with Islamic injunctions. It had a casual attitude toward religion and its caliphs. Abd al-Malik (685–705) was an exception to this and he laid great emphasis on the building of mosques. Its power moved westward through Spain and into southern France. Muslim kings marched eastward to Central Asia, Eastern Persia, and borders of Afghanistan and India.

The rulers of the Abbasid Dynasty (750–1258) emphasized on traditions of Islam, calling themselves 'blessed dynasty'. This age is also called the Golden Age of Islamic civilization. This included vast achievements in mathematics, astronomy, architecture, etc. These rulers supported Islamic studies but their behavior was that of usual kings. Harunal-Rashid and al-Ma'mun were amongst the best known of Abbasid rulers. They had their capital at Baghdad. The second half of the rule of this dynasty witnessed the breakup of the unified Muslim empire and was replaced by territory-based governors. With advent of Christian crusades, the expansion was replaced by defense of the existing empire.

Islam continued in different parts of the world. In Spain (756–1492), it displays a rich blend of Muslim, Christian, and Jewish traditions and cultures. Berbers of North America were one of the early converts of Islam and they maintained their distinct culture all through the period of 750–1269. Fatimids embarked on the attempt to install their own Caliph as the head of Islam (901–1174). Starting from their base in Yemen, they first took control of North Africa and then of Egypt where they built Cairo as their capital. Seljuks and Ayyubids (1055–1243), Mongols (1258–1506), Mamluks (1250–1517), and Ottomans (1326–1683–1924) were other major dynasties of Muslim kings. Ottomans became a major force in the world under Sulayman.

> ...From 1521–1883 the Ottomans constituted one of the greatest empires in the history of the world...their defeat at Vienna in 1683 began the ebb to decline. It ended in dismantling of Ottoman Empire by Allied powers after WWI. The brilliant general Kemal Ataturk (d.1938) restored the fortunes of Turkey, and as a part of secularizing approach he formally ended the Muslim Caliphate in 1924.(Miller 2000, 343)

Muslim kings' rule lasted in India from the 12th to the 17th century. Muslim traders from Gujarat and Malabar brought Islam to Malaysia and Indonesia. Similarly, Islam spread to sub-Saharan regions, and to Europe and America as well. In Europe, it was the constant contact with this religion which helped its spread there, aided by immigration. In America, immigration and conversion of African Americans to Islam were the main causes of the spread of Islam there.

While these countries are called Islamic countries, the kings who ruled these were sitting atop the feudal structures of society; feudal hierarchy of class/caste and gender was the social norm. The hallmark of this mode of production is property being in the hands of feudal nobility.

> From social point of view the feudal lords stood opposed to peasants, the direct producing class, who had no property of their own, but worked on land and were exploited by the feudal nobility through non-economic forms of coercion which varied from outright serfdom to inequality of rights. (Rutenburg 1988, 9)

Though religions identified with the kingdoms, feudal hierarchy was dependent on land rights and was the base of political power of the king, from these kingdoms, which were based on feudalism, modern nation states emerged in due course.

Three major religions, Christianity, Islam, and Buddhism, acquired universal character and provided the basis of law, political theory, and system of ethics. These religions provided a divine authority to the rule of kings. Church, the organized religion, was part of all these religions, irrespective of the religious injunctions of the books and ethics. In practice, the role played by the clergy, through the church, was similar in all the three religious institutions. "There was a division between clergy and laity, the church hierarchy and the principle of authority. They (Clergy) claimed a special place not only in spiritual but also in the life of society" (ibid., 10). Despite core similarities, the social expressions were/are very specific and distinct. The cultural changes related to literary languages and national literature came up during these kingdoms. Absolute monarchy was the hallmark of the kingdoms, including the Islamic ones. These kingdoms came to have distinct boundaries and judicial systems.

Since the WW I, modern reforms have been brought in various Muslim countries to limit the influence of clergy. This pattern is not uniform in different Muslim countries. More so, after the WW II, the newly independent countries of Africa and Asia tried to adopt newer norms of social life. This resulted in modification or abolition of old taboos, the modernization of cults, etc. "In number of countries progressive reforms decisively secularized legal norms and daily life, church land was confiscated, sphere of influence of sharia was limited, the church was separated from the state, and secular schools and higher education was introduced" (Tokarey 1986, 381). After Kemal Atatürk's establishment of republic in Turkey, radical reforms were introduced in full measure.

What is known as the Muslim world was the kingdoms of different hues and colors. Kingdoms all over had a particular political structure. In that, the king was the repository of divine power and the clergy was the custodian of divine knowledge. It was the clergy who legitimized the rule and divine authority of kings. Sidetracking the morals and values of religions, the clergy went on to become the sole symbol, custodian, and representative of religions. It is here that in hindsight the kingdoms are labeled in the name of this or that religion. Kings derived their legitimacy from religious institutions. Even the concept of nation state came much later, but the same concept is pushed back in the history and the present nationalism is seen as a continuation of the past nations. The Industrial Revolution changed the social scene in a thorough manner; it changed the notions of hierarchy, the modes of production and social interaction, and the individual and group identity over a period of time.

By the beginning of the 16th century, almost the entire Arab world came under the domination of the Ottoman Empire. Egypt, Syria, Tripoli, Tunis, and Algiers in the north and Yemen at the southern end of the Arabian Peninsula were incorporated in the empire lorded over by Ottomans. "The Turkish rulers were called sultans and the myth of caliphate, which survived through Mamluke period in Egypt finally vanishes. The ulams once again accepted the new reality and found justification for the Ottoman rule" (Engineer 1994, 82). The Ottoman Empire was "not so much a single community as a group of communities each of which claimed the immediate loyalty of its members. The communities were regional, religious, or to some extent mixture of these" (Hourani 1962, 29). The majority of subjects of the Turkish Empire were Muslims and Arabs. The sultan projected himself as the protector of Islam vis-à-vis Western Christianity. "The Turkish sultan used religion to ensure the loyalty of the Arabs who in one way or the other resented the non-Arab political domination. Earlier Arabs were masters of Islamic empire...for Arabs whatever be the theoretical position, Islam is their national religion" (Engineer 1994, 83).

Many of these areas had to undergo colonial occupation. The colonial period was full of various contradictions. This distorted the whole scene as most of the colonies could not get freedom so easily and the older relations masquerading as religion also persisted. Total democracy has not been the outcome of freedom movements in many countries. The colonial era in most of the countries has left the premodern identities in different measures as a legacy of halfway transition to industrial society. One of the bases of colonial expansion was the discoveries in the areas of science and their application in production technology, leading to the search for markets. The Industrial Revolution in Western countries was not only a new way of production, but it was also the bringing in of newer social values of secularism, pluralism, equality, and all that. But in colonies, and Muslim countries, this was not the case. These values were introduced but not necessarily implemented. Colonies provided raw materials and markets for the colonial masters. At the same time, the native crafts were ruined.

The colonial period was seen by different sections of society in different ways. Some Muslims saw it as a battle of the West invading Islam, some saw it as the crisis of Islam, while some did see it as the newer system of society and production coming in, not under the control of natives but imposed in a distorted, motivated way by the colonial powers. So, in the postcolonial period also, the influence of colonial powers was not totally gone, and democracies were not brought in fully. We will see this in later chapters.

Very few colonies could achieve full democracy after freedom. While many of these went in for socialist, State-controlled economies, many of them inherited problems related to an incomplete secularization process. This led to strife masquerading as ethnic or religious ones. While in countries like Sri Lanka this manifests as a problem between the Sinhala and Tamil identities, in India it manifests as the coming up of Hindutva politics and a matching response in the form of fundamentalist Islamic trends.

Islam in the Political Arena—Wahabism: Salafi Islam

The post-9/11 world has seen the abuse of the word 'Islamic' by associating it with terrorism. The indoctrination of the mujahideen and Taliban was also done by using a particular version of Islam, the Wahabi Islam, and further distorting it toward violence.

Like every other religion, Islam also has many sects and subsects. The Shia, Sunni, Sufi, Wahabi, and Ahmadiya are just a few such examples. Wahabi Islam formed the base on which the CIA further gave it a tilt to prepare the mujahideen to take up arms against the Russian army; later, the same interpretation formed the base for violence against other sects of Islam, and also to intimidate and impose conservative backward norms wherever the writ of Taliban/Al Qaeda ran.

Salafi is a trend in Islam, which stands for the generation of people born immediately after Prophet Muhammad. Their example was presented as the religious norm for later generations. This tendency of Islam called for differentiating 'via media' between the orthodox norms of Islam and secular society and modern science.

The Wahabi tendency of Islam emerged a religio-political movement which came into being at the end of the 18th century in Arabia. An

Arab theologian Muhammad ibn Abd al Wahhab called for the revival of pure Islam. He preached strict monotheism, with no mediators between man and Allah. It rejected worshipping of holy men, and pilgrimage to shrines (*mazars*). The latter is regarded as a compromise with polytheism. They oppose luxury in life, such as smoking, singing, dancing, and drinking. Wahabis regard themselves as the only true Muslims. They stick to the beliefs propounded by the founder of this sect. The version is an extremist one and gives a religious justification for killing those whom they regard as infidels. A large number of Muslims fall in their definition of infidels. It is an extreme interpretation of the Koran and calls for strict obedience to sharia law. It has no place for the interpretation of Islamic laws and does not give any rights to women.

Zubair Murshed summarizes this phenomenon as follows: Salafi Islam began in Arabia, which did not have much diversity. Also, it was more for ideological purity, and such a tendency can lead to extremism with ease. It became the official ideology of Saudi Arabia. Saudi Arabia emerged as a close ally of the United States. Saudi Arabia also spent lots of money to promote this version of Islam. This was the version which was employed in the especially set-up madrassas in Pakistan. The madrassas were the ones where the indoctrination of Muslim youth into the Al Qaeda mindset began.

> The spread of obscurantism amongst followers of various denominations, in recent times, though has emerged as a reaction to or an inspiration from one streak of faith—the Salafism or Wahabism. The Salafism prides itself upon ultra-conservatism, hate-speech and forceful action to prevent vice and spread virtue. In many cases now it calls for achievement of political power to spread faith. (Murshed 2013, http://www.pakistantoday.com. pk/2013/08/08/comment/columns/a-muslim-malaise/#sthash.vhFYOaOD. dpuf [last accessed on October 10, 2014])

It is no coincidence that this tendency of Islam is more prevalent in the sheikhdom of Saudi Arabia. Saudi has been a thick ally of the United States. This Islamist regime of Saudi Arabia is openly practicing and promoting the age-old sharia code beyond its perimeter.

> Although scholars and leaders across the world despise the pre-modern Wahhabism, the state-ideology of the country, the oil-rich monarchy has

love–hate relationship with the West. Ultra-orthodox Wahhabism emerged as an alternative to the colonial Ottoman caliphate which ran the country and the neighboring regions of Iraq–Kuwait and Greater Syria up to the end of World War I. Had there been some space for liberal nationalist movements under the autocratic Turkish caliphate, the more stringent and backward-looking Wahhabis would not have succeeded in establishing what Saudi orthodoxy represents today. The Saudi promotion of Sunni orthodoxy reflects the regime's paranoia about pro-Iranian, anti-monarchical 'Shiite heresy' and the growing Muslim Brotherhood–Iranian understanding. (Roy 1994, 120–21)

Similarly, a very conservative and orthodox version of Islam has been propagated by Maulana Maududi, who became a resident of Pakistan and was the founder of Jamaat-e-Islami. These versions are very close and were picked by the United States for indoctrinating the mujahideen in Pakistani madrassas. These mujahideen later became a part of Al Qaeda.

PART II

Terrorism Today: The View from India

4

Hindutva Terrorism

Terminological Confusions: Hindu or Hindutva

Protests were organized and threats to stall the proceedings of Parliament session dished out to oppose Home Minister Sushil Kumar Shinde's statement on Hindu terrorism and its links with BJP and RSS (http://www.thehindu.com/news/national/shinde-blasts-bjp-rss-for-inciting-hindu-terror/article4325767.ece [last accessed on January 23, 2013]). There are two major components of this statement. One is the use of the prefix Hindu for terrorism, and the other is about the RSS–BJP links with terror training camps. What Shinde called Hindu terrorism has also been called Saffron terrorism or Hindutva terrorism. This prefix is used to point to the acts of terror indulged in by the likes of Sadhvi Pragya Singh Thakur, Swami Aseemanand, Col. Prasad Shrikant Purohit, Kalsangara, Sunil Joshi, and many like them who were either actively associated with the ideology of Hindutva, or were even organizationally associated with RSS. Others were at that time or previously linked with some progeny of RSS, such as ABVP and Bajrang Dal. Many of them were part of organizations such as Sanatan Sanstha and Abhinav Bharat, who again aim at the goal of a Hindu nation or are ideologically inspired by the agenda of RSS.

The Home Minister's remarks were based on investigations done by antiterror squads of different states and by the National Investigation Agency (NIA). Earlier, the announcement was made by the former

Union Home Minister P. Chidambaram, in July 2010, to the Parliament that the NIA would probe the terrorist attacks on the Samjhauta Express and examine the conspiracy behind the attack, including the links of the accused in terrorist attacks at Malegaon (September 8, 2006), at Mecca Masjid in Hyderabad (May 18, 2007), and at Ajmer Dargah (October 11, 2007). He had used the term Saffron terror.

The Terror Phenomenon

Various such acts of terror in which these people have been involved have been coming to light since the last 10 years or so, for example, in 2003, in Parbhani, Jalna, and Jalgaon districts of Maharashtra; in 2005, in Mau district of Uttar Pradesh; in 2006, in Nanded; in January 2008, at the RSS office in Tenkasi, Tirunelveli; in August 2008, in Kanpur, and so on. A few details of some of these acts are very revealing.

1. On April 6, 2006, in the middle of the night, a powerful bomb exploded in a remote place in Nanded, Maharashtra. The house where it exploded belonged to an RSS sympathizer, with the saffron Bajrang Dal flag flying atop the house. There was also a board of Bajrang Dal Nanded Branch on the wall of the house. Fake beards and kurta pajamas were also found there. The impact of the blast could be felt in the whole town, in the perimeter of 2 km; some people felt as if it was an earthquake. In the house where the blast took place, all the furniture was blown apart, two members of Bajrang Dal were killed on the spot, and three others were seriously injured. Unlike crackers, it was a single explosion.

    The case was not well investigated. A Citizens' Inquiry committee investigated the blast. The report pointed out that "...there exist strong indications that deep communal conspiracies were being hatched by Hindutvavadi forces in the city of Nanded" (Khairnar et al. 2010, 121).

2. In Thane on June 4, 2008, two Hindu Jagran Samiti workers were arrested for planting bombs in the basement of Gadkari Rangayatan, Mumbai, India, which injured seven people. The same group was involved in the blasts in Vashi and Panvel, Maharashtra. In one of the few cases of success in investigating such cases in Maharashtra, or anywhere for that matter, the

Anti-Terrorist Squad (ATS) of Police succeeded in nabbing the culprits. As it turned out, this investigation did lead to the real culprits, who happened to be part of Hindu Janajagruti Samiti (HJS), an outfit of Sanatan, Ashram in Panvel. These culprits were also involved in other blasts, in Vashi, Panvel, and Ratnagiri. In Thane, the blasts were done to protest against the play *AmhiPachpute*, a satirical play on the Mahabharata. The allegation was that it insults Hindu gods. The earlier blast in Panvel was in a theater where the film *Jodhaa Akbar* was being screened. In this film, the Hindu princess Jodhaa is married to Akbar, a Muslim king, and that is regarded by these outfits as an insult to Hindu religion (http://articles.timesofindia.indiatimes.com/2010-1221/mumbai/28255225_1_sanatan-sanstha-amhi-pachpute-hemant-chalke).

3. On October 15, 2009, the eve of Diwali, a bomb kept in a scooter went off in Margao, Goa. It killed Malgonda Patil and seriously injured Yogesh Naik. Another bomb was detected in Sancoale in a truck carrying 40 youth for the Narkasur competition. Both the activists belonged to Sanatan Sanstha. The second aim of this blast was to create communal tension in Margao, which has a history of communal violence. This group takes inspiration from Savarkar (Hindu Mahasabha) and Hedgewar (RSS) and indoctrinates its members into hating Christians and Muslims. The ATS of Police succeeded in nabbing the culprits, against whom cases are still going on. It was a clear case of the involvement of Hindu right-wing organizations in a case of terrorism. The culprits belonged to HJS, an outfit of Sanatan Sanstha, whose ashrams is based in Panvel near Mumbai. These culprits were also involved in other blasts, in Vashi, Panvel, and Ratnagiri.

   The "blast went off in a scooter (bearing no GA 05 A 7800) behind the grace Church at around 9.45 PM…. The duo riding the scooter were, in fact following the effigy of a Narkasur, which was coming down the grace Church road from Gayling" (Gatade 2011, 204).

4. On August 24, 2008, two Bajrang Dal activists died in Kanpur, while making bombs. The Kanpur zone Inspector General of Police (IGP) S.N. Singh stated that their investigations had

revealed that this group was planning massive explosions all over the state. "Twelve suspects, under the scanner in connection with the Kanpur blast, had links with the two Bajrang Dal activists who died in the blast, Bhupinder Singh Chopra and Rajiv Mishra" (ibid., 178). Gatade also points out that the police had tried to unearth the interconnections between the Kanpur blasts and the Kannur blasts in Kerala.

5. The *Indian Express*, October 23, 2008, reports that those involved in the bomb blasts in Malegaon and Modasa (September 2008) had links with ABVP. Similarly, in Tenkasi, Tamil Nadu, a pipe bomb attack on the RSS office (January 2008) was projected to have been done by Jehadi Muslims.

The common pattern of these acts of terror has been twofold. First, in a few of such cases, the activists related to Bajrang Dal or fellow travelers were killed while making the bombs. Second, these acts of terror were targeted to kill the Muslims, so these acts were organized at times when the Muslim congregations were taking place, at the time of *namaz* (prayer) or festivals like *Shab-e-Barat* in Malegaon, or in Ajmer Sharif where they come in large numbers, or the Samjhauta Express where the major number of travelers are Muslims.

While in the initial phase police authorities working under the prejudice that 'all terrorists are Muslims' misdirected their probe, the probe came on the proper track after the Malegaon blasts when the motorcycle of Sadhvi Pragya Singh Thakur, the former activist of ABVP, a wing of RSS, came under the scanner and her links with many of those who have been named above and are currently in jail came to the surface. These facts came to light due to the initiative taken and immaculate investigation done by the then Chief of Maharashtra ATS, Hemant Karkare. Karkare pursued the investigation professionally, putting together the threads due to which today most of them are in jails. While pursuing these investigations, Karkare came under immense pressure from the politicians belonging to BJP and its close cousin, Shiv Sena. During this time, Narendra Modi said that Hemant Karkare is an antinationalist (*deshdrohi*) and Bal Thackeray in his *Saamna* wrote, "We spit on the face of Karkare." Later, Karkare was killed in the Mumbai terror attack of 26/11 November 26, 2008. The people involved in some way were associated with the affiliates of RSS or RSS itself. Mr R.K. Singh, Home Secretary, has given some of the names from the RSS stable who have been allegedly involved in acts of terror.

1. Sunil Joshi (dead): He was an 'activist of RSS' in Dewas and Mhow from the 1990s to 2003.
2. Sandeep Dange (absconding): He was 'RSS pracharak' in Mhow, Indore, Uttarkashi, and Sajhapur from the 1990s to 2006.
3. Lokesh Sharma (arrested): He was 'RSS nagarkaryavahak' in Deogarh.
4. Swami Aseemanand (arrested): He was 'associated with RSS wing Vanavasi Kalyan Parishad' in Dangs, Gujarat, in the 1990s to 2007.
5. Rajender alias Samunder (arrested): He was 'RSS VargVistarak'.
6. Mukesh Vasani (arrested): He was an 'activist of RSS' in Godhra.
7. Devender Gupta (arrested): He was an 'RSS pracharak' in Mhow and Indore.
8. Chandrasekhar Leve (arrested): He was an 'RSS pracharak' in Shajhanpur in 2007.
9. Kamal Chouhan (arrested): He was an 'RSS activist'.
10. Ramji Kalsangra (absconding): He was an 'RSS associate'.

(http://indiatoday.intoday.in/story/government-releases-names-of-hindutva-terrorists-nia/1/247201.html)

This is in addition to Sadhvi Pragya Singh Thakur, Swami Dayanand Pandey, Lt. Col. Prasad Shrikant Purohit, and retired Major Upadhyay, who have been close to them.

While some beans were spilled by many of these accused, the whole picture was pieced together by Swami Aseemanand, when he decided to confess in front of the magistrate. In his confession, Swami gave the details of the whole setup raised under his coordination and involving many RSS workers and their associates. The major reason for this whole planning, as per him, was to counter the Islamic terrorism as witnessed in the Sankat Mochan temple, etc., and the second goal was to pave the path of a Hindu nation.

The later investigation of the ATS and now NIA has unearthed the linkages due to which these activists are cooling their heels in jails.

Meanwhile, in the wake of most of these terror blasts, many Muslim youths were arrested, some of whom were later released for the lack of any credible evidence. So this whole series of terrorists are Hindus. Does this then justify to label this type of terrorism as Hindu terrorism? By no means! Shinde is wrong to label this terrorism as Hindu terrorism.

Is the term 'Saffron terrorism' correct? No way. This term was used by many including the then Home Minister P. Chidambaram in the wake of the investigations done by Hemant Karkare in the case of Malegaon blasts. While one does not approve the term Hindu terrorism or Saffron terrorism at all, one would like to see the background in which this term came to be used. The RSS routinely adopts resolutions seeking to "curb Islamic terrorism with an iron hand." The term Islamic terrorism was first coined by American media in the light of the 9/11 act of terror. This was the first major attempt to label an act of terror with religion. This became the most popular word, and all and sundry resorted to this word time and time again. This was a deliberate mischief by the United States to target the Muslims and thereby get legitimacy to launch attacks in West Asia to control their oil resources. In India also, a large section of the media picked it up. RSS and its progeny in particular highlighted the religious nature of this terrorism, and the word *jihadi* terrorism was a common term in use. In a way, associating terrorism with religion became a dominant norm and a part of popular perception.

In this backdrop, when the acts of terror done by many Hindus came to light, they somehow came to be labeled with the prefix es 'Hindu' or 'Saffron'. The terms Islamic terrorism or *jihadi* terrorism are as wrong as the terms Hindu terror or Saffron terror. The right word for the former may be Al Qaeda terrorism and for the latter Hindutva terrorism. Here again, the term Hindutva terrorism is fraught with misunderstanding. As such, Hindutva is a politics aiming at the creation of a Hindu nation, but due to its containing the word Hindu in it, it is also taken to be a religion in popular understanding. So the dilemma for Shinde! How to label this group of terror deeds? Probably, one will like to make it clear that it is Hindutva terrorism, it has nothing to do with the Hindu religion, and the difference between the terms Hindu (religion) and Hindutva (politics) needs to be made clear in popular parlance.

So it smacks of hypocrisy when noise when the word Hindu–Saffron terrorism is used. The same set of people are using the term Islamic terrorism or *jihadi* terrorism and propagating that all terrorists are Muslims. One has to know that the phenomenon of terror has been promoted in the madrassas specially set up by America in Pakistan to indoctrinate the Muslim youth and bring up Al Qaeda-type formations. So why demonize Islam, Muslims, and use the term *jihadi* terrorism? Both such abuses of religion run parallel to each other.

What about the statement about training camps run by RSS and BJP? In all fairness, one conceded that the training camps run by RSS provide training in rifles but the training centers of bomb-making and use are not directly run by RSS–BJP. Surely, these activities are done by those associated with RSS–BJP. One cannot take lightly the picture circulating in the social media, which shows Rajnath Singh and Shivrajsingh Chowhan with Sadhvi Pragya Thakur. One also cannot dismiss the fact that Lal Krishna Advani and Sushma Swaraj had gone to see the Prime Minister to plead the case of Pragya Singh Thakur in particular. One cannot ignore that those running these training camps had or were associated with RSS in some way, actively at that time or in the past.

So all these protests and threats of BJP, and threats to disrupt the session of Parliament, are their usual political tactics and do not have any meaning, as their indirect or direct association with the terrorists is quite obvious. What Shinde is stating is factual, but the terminology is confused, and that is not due to his own fault. We as a society have not been able to coin correct terminologies for different acts of terror anyway, so why get away with using the word *jihadi* terrorism and haul Mr Shinde to the coals for such a use of the term?

Two Major Cases of Blasts by Hindutva Groups

Malegaon Blast

A blast occurred in Malegaon in the *kabristan* (graveyard), which is near a mosque. It was Friday, September 8, 2008, at 1.15 p.m., just after the prayers. This was a Shab-e-Barat holiday so the crowd was big. In this blast, 37 people died and 125 were injured. Most of the people who died were Muslim pilgrims. The police investigators blamed SIMI for the blast. One person, Noor-ul-Hooda, was alleged to be a part of SIMI, and was arrested for the act of terror. By and by, other usual suspects were also named. Shabbir Batterywala was named as a part of the dreaded Lashkar-e-Taiba, and Raees Ahmad was arrested as co-conspirator; he was tagged with SIMI. While there was a murmur that Hindutva organizations may be involved, the authorities ruled it out on the grounds that the type of explosives, RDX, that were used were not available with Bajrang Dal, etc.; the type of bomb used in Malegaon was too sophisticated for Bajrang Dal, and also that they do not have such organizational capability. While the police pointed out that the pattern of these blasts was similar to the one which occurred in other mosques in Maharashtra, the Bajrang Dal was still not suspected. Confessions were elicited under coercion from the accused. They denied the charges in front of magistrates and no further headway could be made; there was no concrete proof.

In Malegaon, another blast took place two years later. The low-intensity blast took place in the crowded Bhikku Chowk in Malegaon at a time when people were breaking their Ramadan fast. Initially, the police thought that it was the blast of a gas cylinder, but later confirmed that the blast took place due to a device tied to a Hero Honda motorcycle. This investigation was conducted by Hemant Karkare of Maharashtra ATS, who was later killed in the Mumbai 26/11 attack. The investigation put Sadhvi Pragya Singh Thakur, Swami Dayanand Pandey, serving army officer Lt. Col. Prasad Shrikant Purohit, and retired army officer Maj. Upadhyay behind the bars. Subhash Gatade points out: "A day after the Maharashtra police said it could not rule out the possibility of Hindu extremist hand in Monday's blast in Malegaon, investigators are revisiting the crude bombs that were planted in auditoriums on the outskirts of Mumbai earlier this year." The ATS is planning to interrogate the activists of HJS, Sanatan Sanstha, and other stray Hindu extremist organizations for their possible involvement in the act (Malegaon, Modassa, and Mehrauli Blasts, cited in Gatade 2011, 34).

Mecca Masjid Blast

The second case is that of the Mecca Masjid blast in Hyderabad on May 18, 2007, at the time of *namaz* prayers in the afternoon. At that time, thousands of people were in the mosque. Further, the police as usual raised fingers at Harkat-ul-Jihad-al-Islami or HUJI and the SIMI as the main suspects behind the Friday Mecca Masjid blast. Nearly 25 Muslim youth were arrested alleging different affiliations, but all of them were released after six months for the lack of evidence. In both Malegaon and Hyderabad Mecca Masjid, like many other places, what is evident is that Muslims had been the main victims and later the main suspects, confirming the path taken by officials that all terrorists are Muslims, which has been their line of thinking in all cases of blasts.

For Indian investigation authorities, after every act of blast the suspicion is on a foreign link (i.e., Pakistan, HUJI, Lashkar-e-Taiba mujahideen, etc.). There was an instant response from the authorities in naming the culprit. While at some places it may have been true, but beyond a point it became a knee-jerk understanding after any terror act. And as an accomplice or as the executer in its own right, SIMI kept figuring most of the times.

Many youths were arrested under this label as the old members of SIMI, after SIMI was banned in 2001. This became a matter of routine after every blast, such as in the cases of Malegaon, Mecca Masjid (Hyderabad), Jaipur, and other places, and was broken after the impeccable proof of Sadhvi Pragya Singh Thakur's motorcycle being found in Malegaon. The motorcycle link led to Swami Dayanand Pandey, Lt. Col. Shrikant Purohit, and many others associated with Hindu right-wing organizations, offshoots of or inspired by RSS ideology.

The society witnessed that after most of the blasts so far, Muslim youth were arrested on the charge of being behind the blasts, were harassed for months, and then released for the lack of evidence. This was more or less a routine pattern and it frightened the whole Muslim community to no end. Many Muslim youths' careers were crushed due to these reckless and baseless arrests. Many minority families underwent severe problems; they were ostracized from their own community once they were dragged into the net on the charges which were guided more by the prevalent biases or stereotypes than any substance. SIMI came to be regarded as the core organization responsible for fomenting trouble through youth. Despite the ban on SIMI in 2001, the Muslim youth kept on being labeled as SIMI activists and put behind the bars.

The ban on SIMI was challenged; so a tribunal had to be appointed to review the ban. Ajit Sahi of *Tehelka* in his painstaking investigation followed the tribunal's sitting all through (*Tehelka*, SIMI Fictions, August 12, 2008; http://archive.tehelka.com/story_main42.asp?filename=Ws080809Ram_Puniyani.asp); the tribunal did not find any evidence of the charges put against the organization for banning it. The ban could not be upheld. About this investigation, Ajit Sahi said,

> ...his investigation is no dry story rising from lifeless court documents. It has been an emotional roller coaster to sit across young boys barely into manhood, their foreheads creased by sleepless nights worried stiff over the jailing of a father, a brother, wondering endlessly, "Will this end? Is this for real? What do I do now? Where do I go now? Will I survive this?"

He further says, "As I interviewed countless Muslims, so weathered, I couldn't but ask myself, What if this was me? What if it was my brother, my father in jail?" Ajit Sahi presented his travails to find out about SIMI at the tribunal. It was one of the peak points of the tribunal.

With the world scenario tilting against Islam and Muslims, courtesy the radical Islamists trained in the Madrassas set up in Pakistan with US aid, the popular psyche perceived an average Muslim as a terrorist and police machinery operated on this understanding. Even when scores of lives were shattered and the community came under intimidation of the highest order, the government did not take any measures to correct this pattern of investigation with which the police was pursuing its work.

The Hindutva groups came under the scanner with the Nanded bomb blast in the house of Bajrang Dal workers who were making bombs (http://www.frontline.in/static/html/fl2524/stories/20081205252411200.htm [last accessed on October 10, 2014]).

Excerpts of the Confession by Swami Aseemanand to the Metropolitan Magistrate of Delhi, as Reported by *Tehelka*

> Sir, when I was lodged in Chanchalguda district jail in Hyderabad, one of my co-inmates was Kaleem. During my interaction with Kaleem I learnt that

he was previously arrested in the Mecca Masjid bomb blast case and he had to spend about one and a half years in prison. During my stay in jail, Kaleem helped me a lot and used to serve me by bringing water, food, etc. for me. I was very moved by Kaleem's good conduct and my conscience asked me to do *prayschit* (penance) by making a confessional statement so that real culprits can be punished and no innocent has to suffer.

Indreshji met me at Shabri Dham (Aseemanand's ashram in the Dangs district of Gujarat) sometime in 2005.

He was accompanied by many top RSS functionaries. He told me that exploding bombs was not my job and instead told me to focus on the tribal welfare work assigned to me by the RSS. He said he had deputed Sunil Joshi for this job (terror attacks) and he would extend Joshi whatever help was required.

The Muslim terrorists started attacking Hindu temples in 2002. This caused great concern and anger in me. I used to share my concerns about the growing menace of Islamic terrorism with Bharat Riteshwar of Valsad.

In March 2006, Pragya Thakur, Sunil Joshi, Bharat Riteshwar and I decided to give a befitting reply to the Sankatmochan blasts.

I told everybody that *bomb ka jawab bomb se dena chahiye* (I told everyone we should answer bombs with bombs). At that meeting I realised Joshi and his group were already doing something on the subject.

After the combined meeting, Joshi, Pragya, Riteshwar and I huddled together for a separate meeting. I suggested that 80 percent of the people of Malegaon were Muslims and we should explode the first bomb in Malegaon itself. I also said that during the Partition, the Nizam of Hyderabad had wanted to go with Pakistan so Hyderabad was also a fair target. Then I said that since Hindus also throng the Ajmer Sharif Dargah in large numbers we should also explode a bomb in Ajmer which would deter the Hindus from going there. I also suggested the Aligarh Muslim University as a terror target.

In the meeting, Joshi suggested that it was basically Pakistanis who travel on the Samjhauta Express train that runs between India and Pakistan and therefore we should attack the train as well. Joshi took the responsibility of targeting Samjhauta himself and said that the chemicals required for the blasts would be arranged by Dange.

Joshi said three teams would be constituted to execute the blasts. One team would arrange finance and logistics. The second team would arrange for the explosives. And the third team would plant the bombs. He also said that the members of one team should not know members from the other two teams. So even if one gets arrested the others would remain safe.

Joshi came to see me at Shabri Dham on Diwali in 2006. The Malegaon blasts had already happened. Sunil told me the blasts were carried out by our men. I said the newspaper reports had mentioned that Muslims were behind the blasts and a few Muslims had also been arrested. Sunil assured me the blasts were carried out by him but he refused to reveal the identity of our men who had executed the blasts.

In February 2007, Riteshwar and Joshi came on a motorbike to a Lord Shiva temple in a place called Balpur. As we had fixed this place for our meeting, I was already there, waiting for the two. Joshi told me in the next two days there would be a piece of good news and I should keep a tab on the newspapers. After the meeting I came back to Shabri Dham and Joshi and Riteshwar went their way. After a couple of days I went to meet Riteshwar at his Valsad residence. Joshi and Pragya were already present there. The Samjhauta Express blasts had happened. I asked Joshi how he was present there while Samjhauta had already happened in Haryana. Joshi replied that the blasts were done by his men.

In the same meeting, Joshi took Rs 40,000 from me to carry out the blasts in Hyderabad. A few months later, Joshi telephoned me and told me to keep a tab on the newspapers as some good news was in the offing. In a few days the news of the Mecca Masjid blast appeared in the papers. After 7–8 days, Joshi came to Shabri Dham and brought a Telugu newspaper with him. It had a picture of the blast. I told Joshi that in the papers it had appeared that some Muslim boys had been rounded up for the blast. But Joshi replied it was done by our people.

A couple of days after the Ajmer blast Joshi came to see me. He was accompanied by two men named Raj and Mehul who had also visited Shabri Dham on previous occasions. Joshi claimed his men had perpetrated the blast and he was also present at Ajmer Dargah at the time of the blast. He said that Indresh had provided him two Muslim boys to plant the bomb. I told Joshi that if the Muslim boys get caught, Indresh would get exposed. I also told Joshi that Indresh might get him killed and told him to stay at Shabri Dham. Joshi then told me that Raj and Mehul were wanted in the Baroda Best Bakery case (12 Muslims were killed by rioters in Best Bakery in Gujarat 2002). I told Joshi not to keep Raj and Mehul at the ashram as it would not be safe for them to stay in Gujarat. Joshi, along with the two men, left for Dewas the next day.

I participated in many Abhinav Bharat meetings and proposed to carry out more terror strikes.

Sometime in October 2008, Dange phoned me and said he wanted to come to Shabri Dham and stay there for a few days. I told him that since I was setting out for Nadiad (Gujarat), it would not be a good idea for him to stay there in my absence. Then Dange requested me to pick him up from a place called Vyara and drop him to Baroda which was on the way to Nadiad. I picked up Dange from Vyara bus stop in my Santro car.

He was accompanied by Ramji Kalsangra. Both were carrying two or three bags stuffed with some heavy objects. They told me they were coming from Maharashtra. I dropped them at Rajpipla junction at Baroda. I later realised that it was just a day after the Malegaon blast. (http://archive.tehelka.com/story_main48.asp?filename=Ne150111Coverstory.asp)

Swami Aseemanand and the Art of 'Statement Withdrawal'

Swami Aseemanand emerged as the alleged kingpin in the series of blasts, starting from Malegaon, Mecca Masjid (Hyderabad), Ajmer Dargah, and Samjhauta Express, which rocked the nation from 2006 onward. Just to recall, the initial investigations into the series of blasts allegedly done by Hindutva groups were led by Hemant Karkare, who was later killed in the 26/11, 2008, Mumbai terror attack. Later, Rajasthan ATS took over and the long trail of investigation that led to unearthing the network of the Hindutva activists inspired by the ideology of Hindutva and working for different groups close to or associated with RSS. Many of them are currently in jails. Recently, Swami and three others have been formally charged (January 25, 2014) in the Samjhauta Express blast, Swami being the primary accused.

After his arrest, Swami confessed to his crimes in front of a metropolitan magistrate. The confession was voluntary, recorded under Section 164 of the Criminal Procedure Code before the metropolitan magistrate Deepak Dabas at Tis Hazari court on December 18. Swami had refused legal assistance and the statement was recorded after 48 hours of judicial custody, to ensure that no sort of pressure or intimidation was working on the mind of the confessor. In this statement, he confessed that he and other Hindu activists were involved in bombings at Muslim religious places because they wanted to answer every Islamist terror act with 'a bomb for bomb' policy. This was a 42-page confession and was widely reported in the media.

A bit later, he retracted the statement saying that it was given under coercion. This came as a lot of surprise as one knows that the statements given in front of police authorities can be under pressure or coercion but in front of a judge it is another matter. His 48 hours' judicial custody was a time enough to consider all aspects of the issues involved. It seems more of a turning around, an afterthought to protect his associates and the parent organization. It reminds one of the statement of Nathuram Godse in the trial of Gandhi's murder that he had no links with RSS. Later, his brother, Gopal Godse, said in an interview that the denial of their links with RSS was deliberate to protect their colleagues in that organization (http://www.frontline.in/books/the-bjp-and-nathuram-godse/article4328688.ece [last accessed on October 10, 2014]). Swami, after accepting the legal assistance, retracted his statement.

There seems to be a repeat performance on his side. Once his interviews were published in *Caravan*, a lot of turmoil was created. Immediately, Swami went on to retract his content of the interviews he gave to the reporter. The reporter and the editor of the magazine have stood by their version and have also released parts of the audio tapes to authenticate the interview's contents. This *Caravan* story not only reconfirmed most of what Swami had confessed in the court but also added other dimensions. The said article is very explosive as it takes the terror link right to the top of the RSS organization head. The *Caravan* report points out:

> ...[A]seemanand's description of the plot in which he was involved became increasingly detailed. In our third and fourth interviews, he told me that his terrorist acts were sanctioned by the highest levels of the RSS—all the way up to Mohan Bhagwat, the current RSS chief, who was the organization's general secretary at the time. Aseemanand told me that Bhagwat said of the violence, "It's very important that it be done. But you should not link it to the Sangh...."
>
> Aseemanand told me about a meeting that allegedly took place, in July 2005. ...In a tent pitched by a river several kilometers away from the temple, Bhagwat and Kumar met with Aseemanand and his accomplice Sunil Joshi. Joshi informed Bhagwat of a plan to bomb several Muslim targets around India. According to Aseemanand, both RSS leaders approved, and Bhagwat told him, "You can work on this with Sunil. We will not be involved, but if you are doing this, you can consider us to be with you." (Reghunath 2014, http://www.caravanmagazine.in/reportage/believer [last accessed on October 10, 2014])

In this report, the writer Leena Gita Reghunath tells us that she met Swami four times over a period of two years and talked to him at length. This detailed account elaborates on the activities of Swami Aseemanand, who was part of Vanvasi Kalyan Ashram, which is an RSS associate organization. Aseemanand is a trained RSS *swayamsevak* (volunteer) who undertook work in the *adivasi* areas and was the main person to organize the Shabri Kumbh in Dangs. He makes his agenda clear in a very explicit way. His goal was to bring *adivasis* into the Hindu fold through a process of *gharvapasi* (returning home). He was not interested in their real issues as such. The issues of *adivasis*, those related to their welfare and their rights, did not matter at all. I too recall that as a member of the concerned citizens group, while visiting Swami's ashram, one could see the malnourished, semi-clothed *adivasi* children shouting "Jai Shri Ram" to our team which was studying the phenomenon of the planned Shabri Kumbh. Some parts of the story carried out by *Caravan*, related to his work in *adivasi* areas and his being the core organizer of the Shabri Kumbh, has earlier been reported by a section of the media, as well as the inquiry reports which went on to investigate the attacks on Christians in the area of Dangs. Many of these facts are spilling out from the horse's mouth now.

The other highlight of the *Caravan* story is the pride with which Swami declares that all this is a part of his political agenda. He is also proud that he is in the same jail cell in which Nathuram Godse was lodged before his hanging. During the course of his interview, he also confesses that he hosted planning sessions, selected targets, provided funds for the construction of improvised explosive devices, and sheltered and otherwise aided those who planted the bombs. This was part of his confession to the metropolitan magistrate as well.

As per Aseemanand:

> Bhagwat said of the violence... If you do it, then people won't say that we did a crime for the sake of committing a crime. It will be connected to the ideology. This is very important for Hindus. Please do this. You have our blessings.

Now the whole thing will lapse in the quagmire of the authenticity of the interview, the forensic test of the tapes, and what not. If Swami could retract the statement given to the magistrate, disowning the interview is no big game. This aspect of the alleged RSS-related activities needs to be thoroughly and professionally investigated irrespective of the stature of those directly or indirectly involved in the acts of terror.

Hindutva Terror: Chronology

1. **Cheruvanchery Blast, Kerala, November 11, 2008**: Similar to the Nanded blast. Two RSS men died while assembling a bomb. Later on, 125 more bombs were found from the surrounding areas.

2. **Assam, October 30, 2008**: At least 45 were killed (figures vary) and over 100 injured in 18 terror bombings across Assam.

3. **Imphal, October 21, 2008**: 17 were killed in a powerful blast near the Manipur Police Commando complex.

4. **Kanpur, October 14, 2008**: Eight people were injured after a bomb planted on a rented bicycle went off in the Colonelganj market.

5. **Malegaon, Maharashtra, September, 2008**: Five people died after a bomb kept in a motorbike went off in a crowded market.

6. **Modasa, Gujarat, September 29, 2008**: One person was killed and several injured after a low-intensity bomb kept on a motorcycle went off near a mosque.

7. **New Delhi, September 27, 2008**: Three people were killed after a crude bomb was thrown in a busy market in Mehrauli.

8. **New Delhi, September 13, 2008**: 26 people were killed in six blasts across the city.

9. **Ahmedabad, July 26, 2008**: 57 people were killed after 20 odd synchronized bombs went off within less than two hours.

10. **Bangalore, July 25, 2008**: One person was killed in a low-intensity bomb explosion.

11. **Thane Blast, June 4, 2008**: A bomb went off in the parking lot of a theater in Thane.

12. **Jaipur, May 13, 2008**: 68 people were killed in serial bombings.

13. **Ajmer, October 2007**: Two were killed in a blast inside the Ajmer Sharif shrine during Ramadan.

14. **Hyderabad, August 25, 2007**: 42 people were killed in two blasts, at a popular eatery and a public park.

15. **Hyderabad, May 2007**: A bomb at Mecca Masjid in Hyderabad killed 11 people.

16. **Samjhauta Express, February 19, 2007**: 66 people were killed, most of them Pakistanis, after two firebombs went off on the India–Pakistan friendship train.

17. **Malegaon, Maharashtra, September 8, 2006**: On Friday, 40 people were killed and 100 injured in a twin blast at a mosque in Malegaon.
18. **Mumbai, July 11, 2006**: 209 people were killed in seven blasts on suburban trains and stations.
19. **Nanded, April 6, 2006**: Two RSS people were killed while assembling a bomb.
20. **Varanasi, March 7, 2006**: 21 people were killed in three blasts, including one at a temple and another at a railway station.
21. **New Delhi, October 29, 2005**: 61 people were killed in three blasts on the eve of Diwali.
22. **Jalna, August 27, 2004**: On Friday, at the Quadriya Masjid, Sadar Bazar.
23. **Purna, August 27, 2004**: On Friday, at the Meraj-ul-Uloom Madarsa and Masjid, Siddharth Nagar.
24. **Parbhani, November 21, 2003**: On Friday, at Mohammadiya Masjid, Rehmat Nagary.
25. **Parbhani, 2003**: Gosiya Masjid. Exact date not available. Very few articles on the Internet have this reference.

(http://faketerrorism.wordpress.com/chronology-major-terrorist-activities-in-india/ [last accessed on October 10, 2014]).

5

From Hindu, Hinduism, to Hindutva

The Roots of Terror

The Hindutva terror bases itself on the goal of 'Hindu *rashtra*, (Hindu nation). This in turn draws its identity from the Hindu religion, which is a collation of different religious tendencies prevalent in this part of the world. Hinduism, as a religion, does not have a founding prophet as it is the bringing together of different religious streams under one umbrella. The acts of terror done by those owing allegiance to the notion of Hindu rashtra are rooted in the politics of the Hindutva and Brahmanical streams of Hinduism.

Today's social common sense believes Hinduism to be the religion of all the people in India except those who are specifically Muslims or Christians. It will be interesting to note that contrary to the popular belief, the terms Hindu and Hinduism originated at different points of time. The term Hindu originated as a geographical term for all those living on the east bank of the river Sindhu. Those coming from Iran, West Asia, had coined this term as in their language the letter H is used more often than the letter S. Much later, this term was bestowed with a religious meaning. In the late 18th century, the word Hinduism became more rooted and was used by British administrators. They believed that "the essence of India existed in a number of key Hindu classical scriptures such as Vedas, the codes of Manu and the *shastras* that often prescribe hierarchical ideas...," a conclusion "supported and elaborated by Brahmans" (Douglas and Prakash 1991). The British not only absorbed this understanding, but also put an official seal on it "by applying a legal system based on Brahmanic norms to all non-Muslim castes and outcastes, and created an entirely new Brahman legitimacy. They further validated Brahman authority by employing, almost exclusively, Brahmans as their clerks and assistants" (Bonner 1994, 40). This fabrication through repetition of "India as unitary Hindu society has obscured the reality of a segmented society, with Brahmans and other upper castes exercising a monopoly of power, fabricated Hinduism is found everywhere" (Bonner 1994, 41).

This historical process whereby Brahmanism gained ascendancy has variously been formulated by different sociologists. To give an example, Arun Bose (1985) writes,

> The ideological and a fortiori social, political and economic development of Indian society was arrested at a primitive nomadic stage by the despotic power of ruthless caste of Brahmin priests who fabricated more successfully than any other priestly caste ever known, myths and legends to deceive, oppress and exploit the remaining castes, particularly the Sudra caste. By draconian punishments, reinforced by legends about creation and the cycle of rebirths through which strict conformity with caste taboos was rewarded and infringements penalized, they were able to enforce total and resigned submission to their omnipotent power.

Nehru (1946) pointed out that

> Hinduism as a faith is vague, amorphous, many sided, all things to all men. It is hardly possible to define it, or indeed to say definitely whether it is a religion or not, in the usual sense of the word, in its present form, and even in the past, it embraces many beliefs and practices, from the highest to the lowest, often opposed to or contradicting each other.

Formulating it more sharply to bring in to focus the caste factor, Hinnells and Sharpe (1972) concede that "a Hindu is a Hindu not because he accepts doctrines and philosophies but because he is a member of 'caste', thus implying that Hinduism is a social order and not a religion." Romila Thapar (1987) in her analysis posits that

> The new Hinduism which is being currently propagated by the Sanghs, Parishads and Samajs is an attempt to restructure the indigenous religions as a monolithic uniform religion, rather paralleling some of the features of Semitic religions. This seems to be a fundamental departure from the essentials of what may be called the indigenous 'Hindu' religions. Its form is not only in many ways alien to the earlier culture of India but equally disturbing is the uniformity which it seeks to impose on the variety of 'Hindu' religions.

Hindu sects are multiple and diverse with many founders, and these sects have survived over a period of centuries. At times, scholars used the word for a group of different indigenous religions, which could vary in their belief system from animism to atheism, which are looked at with suspicion by today's votaries of Hinduism. Thapar (1987) goes on to say,

> Hinduism as defined in contemporary parlance is a collation of beliefs, rites and practices consciously selected from those of the past, interpreted in contemporary idiom in last couple of centuries and the selection conditioned by historical circumstances. In a strict sense, a reference to 'Hinduism' would require a more precise definition of the particular variety referred to Brahminism, Brahmo-Samaj, Arya Samaj, Shaiva Siddhanta, Bhakti, Tantricism or whatever.

The major religious categories, which existed earlier, were Brahmanism and Shramanism. Shramans were those who were often in opposition to Brahmanism; these are the groups which had belief structures different from the Vedas and Dharmashastras. Their teachings transcended castes and communities, and in contrast to Brahmanism, which categorized religious practice by caste, Shramanic religions opposed this in order to universalize their religious teachings. The *bhakti* (worship) tradition emphasized selfless action projected as the need to act in accordance with one's moral duties. This shift of emphasis, away from Brahmanical rites and sacrificial rituals, provided the root, in later time, for a number of cults like *Shaiva, Vaishnava,* and many others. It also provided the rough outlines of much that is viewed as traditional 'Hinduism'. A lot of variations occurred in this tradition. Much later, Kabir and Nanak brought in Sufi ideas in their teachings. Shakta sect and Tantric rituals also gained wide popularity. These are now played down as being anathema to the current version of Hinduism, that is, Brahmanical Hinduism.

The religious practices of untouchables and *adivasis* have a lot of rituals, which involve offerings, and libations of meat and alcohol. Also, these groups could not afford the costly donations required for Brahmanical *yagnas* (rituals around fire). Gradually, *dharma* (religious duty) became central to religion, regarded as sacred, which had to be performed in accordance with one's *varna* (color, occupational hierarchy), *jati* (caste), and sect, and which differed according to each of these. Thapar (1987) goes on to add,

> Hindu missionary organizations, taking their cue from Christian missionaries, are active among the *adivasis*, untouchables and economically backward communities, converting them to 'Hinduism' as defined by upper caste movements of the last two centuries.... That this 'conversion' does little or nothing to change their status as *adivasis*, untouchables and so on and that they continue to be looked down upon by upper caste 'Hindus' is of course of little consequence.

Jainism and Buddhism were major amongst Shramanic tradition. These religions were persecuted in many parts of the country. Premodern Hinduism was not a monolithic religion, as projected by the SP, but was a juxtaposition of multiple religious sects.

Thapar calls the Hinduism currently being propagated by the SP 'Syndicated Hinduism'. This projection is made by the social base of the SP, a powerful urban middle class with a reach to the rural rich who find it useful to bring into politics a uniform, monolithic Hinduism created to serve its new requirement—Hinduism which more or less has taken over the social space and draws mainly from Brahmanical texts, and also from the Dharmashastras. The attempt of this exercise is to present a modern, reformed religion. The net result is a repackaged Brahmanism. The Hindu communities settled abroad look for a parallel to Christianity as their religion. This is to overcome the sense of inferiority and cultural insecurity, which they experience in their life. Thapar goes on to say,

> Syndicated Hinduism claims to be re-establishing the Hinduism of pre-modern times; in fact it is only establishing itself and in the process

distorting the historical and cultural dimensions of indigenous religions and divesting them of the nuances and variety which was a major source of their enrichment.

To put the understanding in a linear way:

> The Hindu religion as it is described today is said to have its roots in the Vedas. In any case, whatever we call the religion of these nomadic clans, it was not the religion that is today known as Hinduism. This (Hinduism in its current version) began to be formulated only in the period of Magadha–Mauryan State, Buddhism and Jainism (as well as the materialist Charvak tradition) were equally old-Hinduism as we know it, was in other words, only one of the many consolidations within a diverse sub-continental cultural tradition, and attained social and political hegemony only during the sixth to tenth century A.D., often after violent confrontations with Buddhism and Jainism. (Omvedt 1995)

As per Gail Omvedt (1995), this Brahmanic Hinduism adopted and identified with the authority of the Vedas and Brahmans. The material base of this system was the caste structure of the society. Its co-optive power was qualified to the extent that dissidents had to accept their place in the caste hierarchy. The masses of people did not have the identity of 'Hindu'. Multiple local gods and traditions existed side by side forming the base of popular culture. Later, only during colonial period was this identity of 'Hindu' constructed for all the inhabitants of this land except those who were followers of Islam or Christianity. This construction was thrown up by the English scholarship and Indian elite. Omvedt posits that

> In the nineteenth century, people like Lokmanya Tilak adopted the 'Aryan theory of Race', claimed a white racial stock for upper caste Indians and accepted Vedas as their core literature. Tilak was also the first to try and unite a large section of the masses around Brahminical leadership with celebration of Ganesh festival.

One gets a clear idea that the SP has succeeded in perpetuating a perception amongst Hindus to forge a communal solidarity through elective projections of the past, and this does involve a deliberate reformulation of history. Emergence of the nation state does bring in a homogenization of religion. In the case of India, this evolution of "national religion and Hinduism has mainly been defined in opposition to the Muslim 'other'."

Hindutva: Ideological Foundations

The construction of Hindutva is to be seen in the backdrop of the emergence of Hinduism as a homogeneous religion. The concept of Brahmanical Hinduism, projected as Hinduism, was at the root of multiple religious revivalist movements. Its political translation began mainly with Bal Gangadhar Tilak, who initiated the Ganapati festival to wean away the popular participation of lower-caste people in the Muharram festival. Some sociologists (Christopher 1993) have called such ideological maneuvers "manipulative reinterpretation of cultural material" and "invention of tradition." Later, Tilak went on to organize a festival in honor of Shivaji, who broke the Moghul hold on western India and opened the way for rampage of Maratha armies through much of India. A strong anti-Muslim slant was brought into function.

Anti-Muslim sentiments were consistently used to project a political methodology of consolidating the Hindus. Starting from Bankim Chandra Chatterjee, various other Hindu national ideologues had whipped the fear psychosis with Muslims as the ones threatening the survival of Hindus. All these fabrications were manufactured and propagated by the ascendant, nascent, amorphous Hindu nationalist forces. The combination of 'syndicated Hinduism' and nationalism was brewed by Vinayak Damodar Savarkar who can be called the first exponent of the doctrine of Hindutva. The mix of Brahmanical Hinduism and nationalism reflecting the interests of the upper castes and a part of the upper class was defined and later refined on the exclusionist principles, which are very basic to the Brahmanism. Savarkar's initial anti-British struggles were very impressive. After assuming the role of the proponent of Hindutva, his major energies were channelized in strengthening the politics of hate, formation of communal Hindu Mahasabha, and helping RSS from a distance.

Savarkar's work *Hindutva: Who Is Hindu* (1923) became and remains the basic text defining this political concept. With the simultaneous rise of Muslim communalism, Muslim nationalism, in due course, most of the Hindu consolidations took place by showing the fear of Muslims. This nationalism consolidated itself on the grounds of the threatening other, but this threatening other was not the British imperialist colonizers because of whose rule the country was suffering but the 'Muslims'. As an aside, we should note here that Savarkar's anti-British struggles and anti-British activities totally ceased after his release by the British, and from then on all his guns were targeted at the Muslims, presented in a most threatening way by him. Savarkar argued (later on, this became the ideological base of most of the Hindutva organizations):

> [T]he Aryans who settled in India at the dawn of history already formed a nation, now embodied in the Hindus.... Hindus are bound together not only by the tie of the love they bear to a common fatherland and by the common blood that courses through their veins and keeps our hearts throbbing and our affection warm but also by the ties of the common homage we pay to our great civilization, our Hindu culture. (Savarkar 1923)

Thus, Hindutva according to him rests on three pillars: geographical unity, racial features, and common culture. He further went on to elaborate the criterion for who is Hindu. According to him, all those who regard this land as their fatherland and holy land are the only ones who are Hindu and thereby the people to whom this land belongs. This led to the automatic interpretation that the Christians and the Muslims, whose holy places are in Jerusalem and Mecca, are not on a par with the 'Hindus' who own this country. This also resulted in the beginning of the theorizing of the 'doubting of patriotism of Muslims'.

Savarkar posits, "But besides culture the tie of common holy-land has at times proved stronger than the claims of a motherland. Look at Mohammedans: Mecca to them is a sterner reality than Delhi or Agra." This development of the concept of Hindutva comes in succession to the construction of Brahmanism as Hinduism, and this Brahmanical Hinduism then forms the base for Hindutva politics. Savarkar began to articulate the ideology of Hindu elite (zamindars, Brahmans, kings) by integrating Brahmanical Hinduism with nationalism, calling it Hindutva, which further showed the way for building the Hindu rashtra. His key sentence was "Hinduize all politics and militarize all Hindudom."

Savarkar's politics were the rival of Gandhian politics. Gandhi, the representative of Indian nationalism, was branded as the conciliator and appeaser of Muslims. Savarkar propounded that struggle for supremacy would begin after the British left and that the Christians and Muslims were the real enemies who could be defeated only by 'Hindutva'. He maintained that this land belonged to Hindus and so by implication Muslims with their holy land in Mecca and Christians with their holy land in Jerusalem cannot have equal status to 'Hindus'. This concept was later to be made more explicit by Golwalkar, who despite adoring Hitler was 'generous' and 'kind' enough to these 'aliens' by granting them the status of second-class citizens. With this began the concept of Hindu Raj—the precursor of the present SP goal—the Hindu rashtra. The final crystallization of Hindutva occurred with the foundation of RSS, which became the father organization for a plethora of organizations, which were to take birth after a period of consolidation of the core *swayamsevaks*.

Hindutva: Growth

The early simmerings of Hindutva can be seen in the opposition to the secular Congress movement of the 19th century. The zamindars (landlords), moneylenders, Brahmans, and *banias* (merchants) spearheaded the reaction to secular politics. This support base constantly stood by the Hindutva politics all through. Later, some industrialists did successfully ride on two boats of supporting the secular Gandhian movement while also supporting the Hindutva movement. But mostly, the modern industrialists stood by the secular movement led by Gandhi. The *rajas* (Hindu kings of Princely States) also by and large stood by the politics of RSS. The march of the industrialization process changed the social composition and brought newer layers into society. Though BJP and its predecessor, the Jan Sangh, began with small electoral support, this support was fairly consistent. It came from the urban middle classes, and sections of the upper castes. Let us have a brief look at the changes in social composition which have occurred during the last 50 years of the republic. The proportion of urban population has gone up by 20–25 percent. They also constitute the ones having derived maximum benefit from modern education and the facilities thrown up by the industrialization process. They do have a sort of dominant presence in the society. The influence cultural, social, and political aspirations of society.

There have been massive changes in the political arena from the late 20th century. The language of political interaction has been made to shift away from the struggles and travails of the poor and exploited, that is, those revolving around bread, butter, shelter, housing, health, and education (the problems of this world). It has been made to take up the issues supposed to be related to 'faith'. We are witness to newer dangers to society, to democratic and secular values in the form of communalism, communal violence, and the rise of new social political forces basing themselves on 'religion' in the political arena. We have been hearing a new word called Hindutva for the last two decades or so. Though this Hindutva ideology has been rooted in certain social segments for the past many decades, its social visibility has increased in the last decade. On first thought, it gives the impression of being some sort of religion. As we will see, it derives its name from the Hindu religion, but it is a political ideology akin to the Islamist political ideology. This political ideology has raised afresh the questions of nationality, community, identity, and a host of other issues in the social space. The Hindutva movement presents itself as an ideal for building a strong nation based on the tenets of 'Hindu dharma', and Hindu rashtra (Hindu nation). There are many notions attached to this word and we need to understand the meaning of this. But this is a newer value system, which has found sympathy amongst a section of the population. We need to understand which segment of society is behind this political movement.

While pursuing its political agenda, the Hindutva movement has brought to the fore a number of precepts, which have found acceptance amongst some sections of society. It has popularized a new version of history, which looks at the past through the parameter of religion alone. Also, the major political force which is the vehicle of Hindutva politics, the RSS, has been spreading this version of history for the past many decades. Today, a large section of the media does accept this version of history. It in a way has become part of the 'social common sense'.

The Hindutva movement is being spearheaded by a plethora of organizations, the patriarch of which is RSS, the real controller of all other organizations. It was founded in 1925 in a backdrop which needs to be understood in detail. In 1920, with the entry of Mahatma Gandhi into the political arena, the dynamics of the anti-British movement got tremendously galvanized. He brought into the struggle people of all religions, castes, and creed. The Brahmanical domination in the Congress started declining. At this time, the upper castes, and the Brahmans, supported by zamindari elements and *banias*, in order to reassert their hegemony on the social political and social scene, came up with the idea of a religion-based national organization, the RSS.

Slightly prior to this, Savarkar put forward the idea of "Hindutva as the basis for politics, which stood for nationalism based on Hinduism" (Douglas and Prakash 1991). At that time, the non-Brahman movement was peaking and threatening to shake the very social power of the zamindar–Brahman nexus. At the international level, the race-based nationalism of the Nazis (Germany) and the Fascists (Italy) was on the ascendance. This was the main inspiration for the ideas of 'nationalism' of RSS.

German National pride has now become the topic of the day. To keep up the purity of the nation and its culture, Germany shocked the world by her purging the country of the Semitic races—the Jews. National pride at its highest has been manifested here. Germany has also shown to the world how well nigh impossible it is for races and cultures having differences going to the roots to be assimilated into one united whole, a good lesson for us in India to learn and profit by. (Bonner 1994, 40)

Marzia Casolari, an Italian researcher who has done work on the roots of Hindu nationalism, concludes that

(a) the main historical organisations and leaders of Hindu Nationalism had a distinctive and sustained interest in fascism and nazism; (b) fascist ideological influences on Hindu Nationalism were present and relevant; (c) to a certain extent, these influences were channeled through direct contacts between Hindu nationalists and members of the Italian fascist state. (Bonner 1994, 41)

RSS decided to keep aloof from day-to-day political struggles and began to train young boys in the doctrine of Hindu rashtra. As per this core ideology of RSS,

Hindus and Hindus alone, constitute the Indian Nation, since they are the original inhabitants and sole creators of its society and culture. Hinduism is uniquely catholic and tolerant and hence superior to other faiths,.... The subsequent entry and takeover by foreigners created an illusion that India was a land of many different and equal cultures.... Only a 'truly secular' Hindu Rashtra will afford protection to non-Hindus. (Bose 1985)

BJP, with its political wing, VHP, is the organization translating Hindutva political agenda on emotive, religious grounds; Bajrang Dal is a group of youths who are active on the streets. Vanvasi Kalyan Ashram is engaged in promoting 'Hindu norms' amongst *adivasis*, and Rashtra Sevika Samiti is its women's wing. In addition, there are other organizations like Saraswati Shishu Mandir, which inculcates in young minds its social, cultural, and political understanding. These all are collectively called the Sangh Parivar (SP).

The initial concern of the Hindutva movement as represented by the Hindu Mahasabha and RSS was to counter the politics of the Muslim League and to influence the Congress in a pro-Hindu direction. RSS was mainly focusing on Shakhas, training volunteers for Hindutva movement, and Hindu Mahasabha was taking part in electoral politics. After Independence, the number of cadres of RSS increased, and Hindu Mahasabha gradually went into oblivion. One ex-pracharak of RSS, Nathuram Godse, murdered Mahatma Gandhi in 1948, following which RSS was banned for some time. Meanwhile, RSS volunteers kept on infiltrating the army, bureaucracy media, and educational institutions. The number of RSS volunteers went on increasing and multiple RSS-controlled organizations started coming up.

RSS undertook mainly campaigns of banning cow slaughter in the 1960s, but the response was lukewarm. It became very visible with its anticommunist propaganda during the India–China war and projected 'nationalist, patriotic' fervor. Its political wing Jan Sanghunder launched the campaign 'Indianize Muslims' in the late 1960s. Meanwhile, the ideology spread by RSS and the increasing urbanization process were the key factors in the increasing intensity of communal violence.

RSS gained higher respectability with the Jaya Prakash movement (1974), and its political wing joined Janata Party, came to power, got vital ministries (external affairs, information and broadcasting, etc.), and used the opportunity to further enter the bureaucracy. It left the

Janata Party on the issue of dual membership. There was a demand from other components of the Janata Party that former members of Jan Sangh leave the RSS, and so, either they should leave RSS or the Janata Party. Jan Sangh did not want to leave the RSS; the Janata Party broke and Jan Sangh reemerged as BJP on the plank of 'Gandhian socialism'.

The early 1980s saw a great turmoil in the society. Initially, the event of conversion of some *dalits* to Islam was projected as the threat of Islam engulfing India. In 1984, Operation Blue Star (Indian army entering the Golden Temple to evacuate the temple from the occupation of Khalistani militants) was followed by the assassination of Indira Gandhi by her bodyguards. This was followed by a massive anti-Sikh pogrom in which many Congress workers led the assaulting mobs. During this pogrom, the RSS ideologue Nanaji Deshmukh wrote a document subtly supporting Rajiv Gandhi's turning a blind eye to the ongoing anti-Sikh pogroms. Later, to appease the Muslim fundamentalists, Rajiv Gandhi got a bill passed in the Lok Sabha to reverse the Shah Bano verdict granting maintenance to her by the Supreme Court. In the same superficial and opportunist style, he went on to get the locks of Babri Masjid opened. Both the fundamentalist streams, Hindu and Muslim, were on the ascendant. The opening of the locks emboldened the Hindu fundamentalists and now the sections of Muslim leadership started feeling insecure on the Babri Masjid issue. Opening of the locks of the Babri Masjid gave a fillip to the SP, and BJP decided to take up the Ram Janmabhoomi issue.

In 1990, due to his own compulsions vis-à-vis the politics of Devi Lal, V.P. Singh cleaned the dust of the Mandal Commission report and decided to implement it. This implementation of the Mandal Commission recommendations intensified the backlash of the upper castes, who rallied around SP in a big way and the Rath Yatra got a tremendous response from these sections of society. With the *Kar Seva* (action aimed to destroy) of December 6, the SP's political wing became politically more powerful, getting more seats in the Lok Sabha and also coming to power in various state assemblies.

After the Babri demolition, massive communal violence followed, more so in Mumbai, Surat, and Bhopal. The polarization of communities along religious lines worsened. This also gave strength to RSS's political child BJP to increase its strength gradually, to the extent that it emerged as the single largest party in 1996 and formed government which lasted for 13 days. Gradually, the other electoral parties, compelled by their lust for power, started allying with BJP, and then BJP led the National Democratic Alliance and ruled for 13 months before coming to power for the full term. Since then, its electoral percentage started declining, but its affiliates such as VHP, Vanvasi Kalyan Ashram, and Bajrang Dal gained strength. It is around this that some affiliates and others inspired by RSS ideology formed suicide squads, set up training centers, and unleashed terrorist violence on the society. Their acts of terror were focused on revenge on the one hand and march toward Hindu rashtra on the other.

PART III

India: A Victim of Global Terror

6

Al Qaeda Strikes:
The Mumbai Terror Attack

On March 12, 1993, the first major terrorist attack occurred in Mumbai in which 13 blasts took place across the city killing 257 people. These blasts took place in the aftermath of the post-Babri demolition carnage. Later, Mumbai also witnessed acts of terror on December 2, 2002, when an explosion took place in a bus in Ghatkopar, the suburb of Mumbai, killing two people. In the backdrop of this was the massive anti-Muslim pogrom in the wake of the Godhra train burning. Similar tragedies shook the city on March 13, 2003, on July 29, 2003, on August 25, 2003, and the last one on July 11, 2006, in the first-class compartments of the Western Railway's local trains. To be more precise, Mumbai has been a victim of acts of terror for the last several years.

The one on November 26, 2008, was of a different nature. It was an operation planned meticulously by a group of jeans–tee shirt-wearing terrorists numbering nearly 10. It seems that they hijacked a Gujarat-registered fishing vessel on the high seas, sailed near Sassoon docks, and reached Gateway of India in dinghies. They were carrying heavy backpacks, and divided themselves into five teams and unleashed mayhem mainly at Chhatrapati Shivaji Terminus (CST), Gokuldas Tejpal Hospital (G.T. Hospital), Metro Cinema, Hotel Taj, Hotel Trident, and Nariman House. Blasts took place at these places and also at Colaba market, Cama Hospital, Nehru Road (Vile Parle), N.B. Road (Malad), and Free Press Road. The attack literally took the breath of Mumbai away for a while:

"…scale audacity, flamboyance and planning of this assault takes one's breath away. As the faces of anonymous, but not hooded, assassins flashed on TV screens, one thing became quickly clear. And what a spectacular success from their perspective, the operation has been" (Mehta 2008). It seems that a lot of preparation had been done to plan this attack: "Mumbai attackers had clearly been trained well; the conspiracy had been in the making for close to a year; ten of the thirty two who had been trained were handpicked for Mission Mumbai and the planning was as detailed as lethal" (Baweja 2009).

The attack left 126 people dead (98 civilians, 14 policemen, and 14 foreigners) and 327 injured. The response to, or the combat against, the terror attack was a very confused affair and is a matter of great concern. One example gives a good idea of the efficacy of response: "The commandos arrived at Taj (Hotel) but declared, in the finest traditions of Indian bureaucracy, that they would not enter the hotel unless they received a written request from the Maharashtra Government" (Sanghavi 2009). Maharashtra ATS Chief Hemant Karkare, who was investigating the Malegaon blasts, was also killed in this episode of violence, along with other top police officials Ashok Kamte and Vijay Salaskar. The Maharashtra Government appointed the Ram Pradhan Committee to look at the role of police in defending the city. The committee released its report on May 26, 2009. The report has not been made public so far, but as per media reports, the report overall exonerates police machinery from any severe shortcomings.

The nation still remembers the 26/11 (2008) tragedy with pain and grief. In this, a group of jeans-clad terrorists rampaged through parts of Mumbai killing over 200 innocent people. The lone survivor from the terrorist group, Ajmal Kasab, faced trial in the courts and was given the death sentence (hanged on November 21, 2012). While tributes were being paid to those who died in the episode and those who laid down their lives while trying to save the nation, some of the old questions raised by this episode remain unanswered, showing the loopholes in the investigation and that the real truth of the tragedy is not out yet. As the facts have been uncovered, it seems that Ajmal Kasab was the handmaiden of players much beyond the easy visibility and reach of Indian agencies. The phenomenon is not just an attack launched from the soil of

Pakistan; it probably has its planners who are not visible easily and who may be beyond the landmass of our neighbor.

The first major question which was raised was about the role of Pakistan. Sections of powers from Pakistan, especially the army, did have a central role to play, as is obvious from some of the clues. It also may be a game between different sections of Pakistani society struggling for supremacy and so clashing with each other within Pakistan. The Pakistani army is trying to maintain its grip over the levers of power, despite the fact that the civilian government is ruling formally. Prior to this incident, Pakistan's President Asif Ali Zardari had extended the hand of friendship to India. The Pakistani army does feel that if the relations between Pakistan and India improve, if a friendship is established between the two nations, the army's dominance in the power equations will go down. Does this observation have something to do with what happened? These are the questions, and the answers to these are a matter of conjuncture. It is important to keep this in mind and not to accuse Pakistan as a whole for what happened. The need is to distinguish between different power centers within Pakistan while firmly dealing with it.

In this sequence, the role of the FBI–ISI agent, David Coleman Headley, was very curious, and quite unmistakeable. Headley's links with the ISI and FBI were there for all to see. So was it a mere game emerging from the soil of Pakistan or were there much bigger players with more sinister plans behind this attack on Mumbai? We hope that one day the truth will come out and the false perceptions will give way to the identification of the real culprits.

The second major point confronting the nation was the death of Hemant Karkare along with two senior officers of the Mumbai police force. Karkare was investigating the case of the Malegaon blast and came across the motorcycle of Sadhvi Pragya Singh Thakur and others, those associated with organizations linked to and inspired by RSS's ideology, some of them being the office bearers of this organization. With Pragya Singh Thakur coming under the scanner, her associates from Abhinav Bharat, Bajrang Dal, etc. also came to light. One of them, Swami Aseemanand, of VHP, was caught, after absconding for long. During the period when Karkare was investigating the links of the Hindutva terror network, some from this camp labeled him as antinational (*deshdrohi*), and one of their leaders went on the say that they spit on Karkare's face! So when Karkare was murdered, there was lot of suspicion about his murder along with two other top police officials.

The then Minister of Minority Affairs, A.R. Antulay, stated that there is terrorism plus something in the whole incident. Antulay was strongly criticized all over and, therefore, he retracted his statement. But the question persisted. The versions of Karkare's death and the gaps in the police version of the incident were too glaring, so the demand came up for an independent probe. The Ram Pradhan Committee was constituted to probe the tragedy. One does not know what the report has to say about the incident as the Maharashtra Government has refused to table the report. Meanwhile, widows of the slain police officers have raised a lot of uncomfortable questions, which have met with silence from the authorities.

The most damning thing on the issue has been the publication of the book *Who Killed Karkare?* by S.M. Mushrif, the retired IGP, Maharashtra (Mushrif 2010). The book is a detailed analysis of the events of the acts of terror which have taken place in Maharashtra. About the 26/11 incident, the book says a lot of things. The major of these have been that the Intelligence Bureau (IB) had prior information about the impending terror attack. During the terror attack there were two teams which were on the job, one caused the major damage to lives, while the other team took the life of Karkare and the other senior police officers. The book has met with stony silence from the state.

Meanwhile, a case has been filed and the Court has asked the Government of Maharashtra to clarify various aspects related to Karkare's murder. One point about this is the intelligence report received a few days before 26/11 warning that Karkare's life was in danger. So the logical question is: What was the response of the government to this information?

What has been instilled in popular perception revolved more around Ajmal Kasab, the small player in the whole game. Questions were asked as to why he was being treated in a royal manner, why he was not being hanged straight away, etc. The norm of a democratic country, the Democratic Constitution, was being bypassed while spreading these types of rumors. Should not the process of law take its own course in all matters related to crime? Why was this propaganda on that Kasab should be hanged straight away? Was it that his deposition might have spilled some other beans which might have been uncomfortable to those spreading such opinions? The whole idea of justice is to ensure that legal procedures are followed to bring out the truth behind the crime. In the case of the Mumbai terror attack, the tragedy is badly confounded as the truth is hidden somewhere and attempts to unravel it do not seem to be satisfactory.

The Mumbai terror attack once more proves that what comes to social awareness is just a tip of the iceberg. Sometimes, what is presented is obvious and the deeper truth remains hidden under the hysterical response. We need to learn a lesson in public life to treat all uncomfortable questions with utmost seriousness and not to be dismissive of the truth hidden in the missing links of the story.

26/11 and Its Probe

Two books by S.M. Mushrif (former IGP, Maharashtra) are:

1. *Who Killed Karkare: The Real Face of Terrorism in India*
2. *26/11 Probe: Why Judiciary Also Failed*

Mumbai has been a victim of terrorist attacks, more so in the aftermath of the ghastly post-Babri demolition violence. The most horrific terrorist attack which shook Mumbai was undoubtedly 26/11, 2008, in which 126 people died and 327 people were injured. It was a terrible episode in which a few young and trained terrorists unleashed a reign of violence. The attack was deadly, and apart from other victims, Hindus and Muslims both, it took away the life of the police officer Hemant Karkare, who was investigating the acts of terror in which the involvement of Hindutva groups was beginning to surface. The police version which was put up had lots of loopholes. The then Minority Affairs Minister A.R. Antulay and many people started having serious doubts about the way the sequence of events were presented by the police. Later, two more glaring things happened: the bulletproof jacket of Hemant Karkare went missing, and his postmortem report was not made public. An intense hue and cry was orchestrated to hang the lone terrorist survivor Ajmal Kasab, and to hang him early. He had the key to unravel some of these queries, and there were elements who wanted him hanged even without a trial.

It is in this background that S.M. Mushrif did a commendable job of putting together all the available evidences and came out with a revealing book, *Who Killed Karkare: The Real Face of Terrorism in India.* In summary, Mushrif challenged the theory put forward by the police and argued that apart from eight terrorists who landed from Pakistan, there were two more who were from the Hindutva groups, who had in collaboration with the IB taken advantage of the knowledge that the terrorists from Pakistan were landing. Instead of alerting the Navy and other concerned authorities, who could have averted the attack, the IB played some other game. Hindutva groups swung into action and planned attacks to eliminate Hemant Karkare, the Maharashtra ATS Chief, whose highly professional investigation had succeeded in nabbing the terrorists belonging to the Hindutva stable. While he was doing his job meticulously, the Hindutva political group Shiv Sena's mouthpiece *Saamna* wrote in the editorial that they spit on the face of Karkare. The present Prime Minister from BJP, Modi, called Karkare antinational.

Mushrif, in an aptly argued book, piecing together all the evidences, demolished the theory presented by the police and proved that "The CST–Cama Hospital–Rangbhavan lane operation was planned, scripted, directed, choreographed, and executed jointly by *Brahiminists* involved in the nationwide terror plot as disclosed in Malegaon blast investigation."

This book upfront challenged the state version seriously. While several editions and multiple translations of the book came out, the IB accused of masterminding the plot kept quiet about the whole thing. No challenging the theory of the book, no banning of the book! The plan might have been to kill the book's theory by ignoring it. A phobia was created to not talk about the theory put forward in the book. The IB seemed to have ensured that this phobia percolated to the judiciary, with the result that the courts ignored many of the crucial facts and arguments raised by the book. Still, though the case ended with the conviction of Ajmal Kasab, a careful scrutiny of the 1,588-page judgment revealed many findings that vindicated the theory of Mushrif. One Mr Radhakant Yadav, a 77-year-old veteran socialist leader of Bihar and a three-time member of the Bihar Legislative Assembly, picked up the threads of the arguments of Mushrif's book and the positive findings of the judgment and filed a criminal writ petition in the Bombay High Court. Important points of the petition are reproduced verbatim in the book under review. The intervention of the court is a major hope in the case, but the state and the concerned authorities are not responding in an adequate manner. The Ram Pradhan Committee report, which went into the role of the police and other authorities concerned in the terror attack, is being kept under wraps. The DVD enclosed in the book also has valuable footage from the TV channels and other sources. One major point shown by the footage is about how Hemant Karkare, the prime target of the 'native conspirators', was trapped.

Surely, Mushrif's both books are crying out for an answer. The popular notions about terrorism have influenced our investigations, thinking, and judgments too far. If the truth is to be unraveled for the sake of national security, an honest examination of the arguments of this book is highly imperative. This book is a powerful indictment of the IB and the Hindutva terrorist groups. Will this stimulate the concerned authorities to give an honest answer?

PART IV

Religion, Politics, and Terrorism

7

Civilizations–Religions:
Clash or Alliance

During the last two decades, the world has seen the rise of politics based on religious identity. Particularly after the 9/11 2001 WTC disaster, there is a widespread feeling that Samuel Huntington's thesis, that after the end of the Cold War, the current time is one of the clash of civilizations (Clash), is true. One has witnessed many controversies where religion has been dragged into the murky world of politics. Osama bin Laden talked of jihad and George Bush responded to the WTC attack by uttering that it was going to be a crusade for him. He and his associate, Blair, both gave divine reasons for the attack on Iraq. A multitude of controversies veered around the Danish cartoons, the Pope's statement on Islam, the banning of *burqa* in some Western countries, and the rise of acts of terror in the name of Islam (http://berkleycenter.georgetown.edu/essays/why-the-west-fears-islam [last accessed on October 10, 2014]), with the epithet that all terrorists are Muslims becoming popular in social thinking in the broad layers of society. Superficially, it was projected as if the clash is between the Islamic culture and the Western civilization. In India also, attempts were made and are underway to project Islam as a religion of violence and Muslims as fanatics out to stick to medieval social norms. The overall impact of the events and the acceptance of this Clash thesis by Huntington have worsened the problem and are widening intercommunity rifts.

The term 'Clash of Civilizations' was put forward by Bernard Lewis and later on converted into a thesis by Samuel Huntington

(http://www.princeton.edu/~achaney/tmve/wiki100k/docs/Clash_of_
Civilizations.html [last accessed on August 28, 2014]) whose essay in a
journal, *Foreign Affairs* (1993), became more popular after 9/11, 2001.
At the end of the Cold War, Francis Fukuyama postulated 'the end of
history', which stood for the belief that:

> What we may be witnessing is not just the end of the Cold War, or the
> passing of a particular period of post-war history, but the end of history
> as such: that is, the end point of mankind's ideological evolution and the
> universalization of Western liberal democracy as the final form of human
> government. (Fukuyama, 1989; https://www.marxists.org/reference/sub-
> ject/philosophy/works/us/fukuyama.htm [accessed on August 28, 2014]).

This was in response to the philosophy of Karl Marx, whose concept of
historical materialism propounded that the struggle between the classes
is the cause of progress of society, leading to a classless society and the
end of history, that is, the beginning of a classless, commune-based society and communism.

In the backdrop of Fukuyama's 'end of history' (ibid.), Huntington
postulated that while the age of ideology (Marxism, classless society) has
ended with the collapse of the Soviet system, the world has only reverted
to a state of cultural conflicts. According to him, the primary axis of
conflict will be along cultural–religious lines.

> It is my hypothesis that the fundamental source of conflict in this new world
> will not be primarily ideological or primarily economic. The great divisions
> among humankind and the dominating source of conflict, will be that the
> cultural. Nation states will remain the most powerful actors in world affairs,
> but the principal conflicts of global politics will occur between nations and
> groups of different civilizations. The Clash will dominate global politics.
> The fault lines between civilizations will be the battle lines of the future.

Many approved of this thesis and the accompanying classification, whose
main criterion is religion. This thesis created anxiety and confusion,
adding to the problems of the nations all around. It is in this context
that Kofi Annan, Secretary General of the UN, launched an initiative, co-
sponsored by the prime ministers of Spain and Turkey, for an Alliance
of Civilizations in August 2005. This initiative nominated a high-level

group, cutting across different religions and nations, to come up with an understanding of the world today and recommend measures to restore the amity of civilizations, cultures, and people of the world. The report was submitted to the Secretary General in mid-November 2006 (http:// www.unaoc.org/repository/report.htm [last accessed on August 28, 2014]), and it is a landmark in more ways than one.

The report debunks the Clash thesis to bring our attention to the alliance between different cultures, nations, and people at all the levels—social, political, and economic. It is not only in current times but since the times people started migrating and interacting that alliance has been the undercurrent of societal life. The report points out that the Clash theory has distorted the terms of discourse on the real nature of the predicament that the World is facing. The history of relations between cultures is not only one of wars and confrontations; it is also based on centuries of constructive exchanges, cross-fertilizations, and peaceful coexistence. One is reminded that India's ex-President, Dr K.R. Narayanan, in response to the Clash thesis, said that civilizations do not clash; it is barbarisms which clash (http://www.krnarayanan. in/html/speeches/others/nov03_99.htm [last accessed on August 28, 2014]). In the Clash thesis, cultures and religions are identified with the religions of the kings, and their wars are presented as clashes between religions or civilizations. The hate ideology spread by communal groups in South Asia also bases itself on the wars between kings of different religions, and these kings are presented as symbols of that religion. The whole aspect of cultural interaction is missing in this discourse. For example, in India, while the atrocities of Aurangzeb are at the core of building the Hate ideology, the confluence articulated by Dara Shikoh, as one can glean through his book, *Majma-Ul-Bahrain*, of India being a confluence of different cultures, is missing in this mindset. Similarly, the rule of Muslim kings in the subcontinent is taken as the point for the legitimization of the Islamic nation.

The worst part of the Clash thesis is that by propagating that cultures are set on a collision course, it helps in turning negotiable disputes into seemingly intractable, identity-based conflicts, and this is what has taken control of popular imagination. The UN report, on the other hand, is based on the multi-polar perspective and the UN Charter of Human Rights. Significantly, it points out that there is no hierarchy amongst cultures as each of them has contributed to the evolution of mankind. While the core problem remains poverty and deprivation of vast sections of mankind, the rising trend of terrorism cannot be dealt with by seeing it as a mere law-and-order problem or having its roots in religion. On the contrary, terrorism itself is a product of political circumstances, which need to be solved on urgent basis. In societies, if some groups are discriminated against, violent repercussions come up and are perceived as liberatory by a section of people, while the same are seen as antinational by the state and other sets of people. The durable solution to the causes of terrorism does not lie in attacking some countries or increasing the role of armed personnel in those areas but in addressing the roots of resentment.

The UN report traces the roots of current violent responses in the partition of Palestine and the formation of Israel, and the latter's occupation of a part of Palestine and other Arab territories, which has come to be seen as a sort of colonialism by a vast mass of people. While Jerusalem remains holy for Jews, Christians, and Muslims, the support of Western powers to Israel's high-handedness is perceived as the collusion of the West with the expansionism of Israel. The committee is very clear on the point that no cause can justify the killing of civilians or noncombatants. It does call for the freedom of religions and takes a strong stand against the desecration of holy places, irrespective of the majority minority religions. The report does recommend several measures in the arenas of education, youth programs, and community actions aimed at promoting alliance, peaking with the recommendation that a forum of alliance of civilizations under the auspices of the UN should be established and this should be promoted at all levels—national, societal, and any other.

The humane spirit of the report is visible all through. However, the point is that in current times, when the very authority of the UN has been undermined by powers that are arrogant, can we look forward to the era of alliance and amity so that the real problems gnawing the vast numbers of human kinds are properly addressed, that is, march in the direction of a better world, that is, struggle for human rights? To put it in another way, is it possible to think positively, to think that "another world is possible," a world where the respect human rights of all of us is adhered to?

Contemporary Times—Role of Religions

Current times are witnessing violence of a severe nature all around in which religion is projected as one of the reasons. It is also projected that violence is a result of a clash between people of two religions and that people belonging to a particular religion are violent due to their faith, and also that some forms of violence are retaliatory violence to check the activities of others who are out to convert gullible people by luring them.

In India, one has seen the intensification of violence in the name of religion, more so over the past two decades. Anti-Christian violence has been the marker of our times. In 1998, a pastor working amongst leprosy patients was burnt alive along with his two innocent sons. After the Babri demolition, a wave of violence rocked the nation. The burning of the Sabarmati Express in Godhra, followed by the massive anti-Muslim violence, the genocide, was another blot on national life. The 9/11 events resulted in the death of close to 3,000 people of all religions. Along with this came the thesis that the current time is one of a clash of civilizations, and that the backward Islamic civilization is out to destroy the advanced Western civilization. One can see the underlining element of the attempt to relate violence and religion in some form or the other.

Along with this came the misunderstanding about other religions. This misunderstanding has assumed mammoth proportions today and it provides the base for the violence and the policy of aggressions/acts of violence and terror. There is a clear need to understand the difference between religion and politics, and to understand the rise of violence from these misconceptions.

Most of the religions came as a set of moral values to guide the people to cultivate the feelings of love for mankind. There began a process of institutionalization of religions to ensure that these values are sustained and percolated to the broad layers of society. At the same time, the emphasis on rituals began to be greater while the focus and emphasis on moral values took a backseat. Over a period of time, the institutional rigidities and rituals, the identity part of religion, have undermined the moral values of religions (http://www.countercurrents.org/puniyani100813.htm [last accessed on August 28, 2014]). There have been numerous attempts to ensure that the basic unity between people of different religions is sustained through the efforts of saints and others who preached the values of humanism in earnest.

Today, vested interests have launched efforts to suppress the weaker section of society and weaker nations for the sake of their material gains. As these attempts are undertaken in the name of religion, a feeling of alienation amongst people overtakes the real spirit of religion.

In India, those associated with the RSS and politics in the name of Hindutva have been spreading hatred amongst different communities. The result is there for all to see. This hate has been spread against both Muslims and Christians (http://twocircles.net/2011dec25/babri_demolition_supporting_anna_hazare_changing_strategies_rss_politics.html [last accessed on October 10, 2014]). Muslims have been projected as fanatics, aggressors, having more than one wife, converting through sword, and being more loyal to Pakistan. This has resulted in a broad social common sense which sees Muslims as the 'other', and ensures their demonization, and the consequent violence at different places even on the smallest of pretexts, which breeds fear and insecurity leading to their ghettoization. At a global level, the United States has been resorting to war against terror which is a ploy to attack areas in oil-rich countries and to create a global Islamophobia. Worldwide, this hatred against Muslims is on the rise. In India, the problem is the worst confounded as the US goals worldwide and RSS goals at home match and worsen the problem. On the other hand, in many Muslim majority countries, similar processes are going on against other religious minorities.

In India, even the tiny minority of Christians has been accused of conversions through allurement and fraud. As a matter of fact, the population of Christians has been declining for the last four decades (1971—2.60 percent, 1981—2.44 percent, 1991—2.32 percent, and 2001—2.30 percent); despite that, sustained scattered attacks on Christian missionaries are on the rise. Similarly, the myths against Muslim minorities have no truth but have captured the minds of people—the destruction of holy places by kings in the past for the sake of power and wealth are being presented as the insult of faith, the conversions in the past are being presented as due to coercion, the demographic profile of the country which is a result of social factors is being shown to be due to religion, the loyalty to other nations is a mere propaganda meant to suit their political goals—and the notion that all Muslims are terrorists also does not hold water as neither is terrorism due to religion nor do all terrorists belong to the Muslim community (LTTE, ULFA, Khalistainis, Irish Republican Army, IRA and so on).

The responsible people of different faiths do realize that this is not in tune with the spirit of their religion. They are watching helplessly this whole process of demonization of certain religious communities and the social rifts being created due to that. Faith in the values of humanism is paramount in the values of religion. The current scenario is pushing back the aspirations of poor people, and so it is needed that the situation be overcome for the sake of a better world, and for the sake of peace and amity. While the political forces bent upon creating this mayhem are very powerful and almighty, and have control over resources of different types as well as on media, the people with genuine faith in human values need to come forward to ensure that this dark phase of human history is overcome in the spirit of dialogue. The need for intercommunity relations and dialogue was never more than in present times.

The isolation, of Muslims, due to this political process is not only creating emotional walls amongst different communities, but also resulting in the retardation of social development. The kernel of present efforts for peace lies in the process of building bridges amongst communities, and that process can be started only by a genuine dialogue amongst people of different faiths, by coming close to each other by abolishing the artificial boundaries created by the politics of hate being practiced by various forces, globally and locally.

These dialogues amongst different religious communities are needed at all levels, starting from the *bastis* (ghettos) and *mohallas* (localities) to the leadership of religions, scholars of religions, the activists engaged in dispelling hate from the society, and those working for human rights—all of them need to be involved in this process of dialogue. The present impasse which is presenting religions as the separating points needs to be overcome with the understanding that religious differences and plural ways of life are a strength, not an obstacle to peace. The dialogue amongst religions needs to be supplemented by cooperation in the field of social work to alleviate the pain and misery of mankind. There is a need for encouragement and coordination in the field of struggles for human rights of deprived sections of society. We aspire for peace and remind ourselves that the peace desired by us cannot be achieved without justice for the people. Justice is a mandatory prerequisite for peace. The spirit of service to mankind has to prevail over the current assault on the basic human values in the name of religion.

We need to look into the recent high-level committee report of the UN which went on to counter the thesis of the Clash put forward by the US professor Samuel Huntington. This thesis forms the cover for the US ambitions for its aggressions in West Asia. The UN committee (http://www.unaoc.org/repository/report.htm [last accessed on August 28, 2014]) has put forward that there is no clash between civilizations; as a matter of fact, civilizations have an alliance for a better tomorrow. On similar lines, one would like to say that there is no clash between the moral values of religions; it is the alliance between these values that the human race can look forward to for a better future, a future which will eliminate poverty, hunger, disease, and misery from the world. Religions should be standing for love and peace. One posits that there cannot be peace without justice, and so the implication is that religions should address the issues not only of poverty but also of the system which creates poverty; it does not talk of just superficial manifestation of the problems but of going to the root of prevalent problems and of raising a voice against perpetrators of injustices. Religions have to raise the issues of human rights of all people of the world. It is this alliance which will ensure that the focus of world policies has to be brought back to the issue of human rights of weaker sections of society. Nothing short of a genuine dialogue amongst people of different faiths can overcome the obstacles created by the political forces misusing religious identity for their political goals.

8

Religion, Power, and Violence

Dharmayudha, Crusade, and Jihad

While currently we are witnessing global politics, the politics for power and pelf using the prefix of religion, it is not that it is a current phenomenon only. The use of religious prefixes for expansionism of kings and even the association of religious establishments, which are popularly perceived as religion, has been fairly old. Barring few patches of history, the use of religious language has been the norm in the secular actions and aspirations of those in power. There have been times when the language of expansion and grabbing power was couched in the civilizing mission of the West, and protection of freedom, etc. from the powers that be; there were also times when the national liberation movements marched forward under the banner of democratic nationalism or socialism. After the decades which saw the maximum number of colonies getting independence from the clutches of imperial powers, and the brief era when imperialists launched their aggression in the name of defense of freedom, the language of crusade, clash of civilization, the threat of a backward Islamic civilizations, and the language of religion are back.

Tribal warfare was entirely of a different nature, small, and for a specific motive. Since tribes did not have the institution of religion, they do not have the paraphernalia of religion as was to follow later; their warfare sometimes evoked their particular gods or goddesses. There are not too many records of these specific instances.

With the emergence of the State as the political institution and with the formation of the clergy as the central figure of the religions, matters changed. In the three major religions of the world, Hinduism, Christianity, and Islam, the specific words for the battles of the kings derive their legitimacy from religious precepts. Wars, the open and most blatant violation of humanity, murders, plunders, and rapes themselves are clothed in holy attire. Many times, the religious institutions and the presiding chiefs of these institutions bless the wars. Even the gods and goddesses of war were conceptualized around that. These gods and goddesses, who are related to war, came into being later than the holy deities of nature.

A peep into the most initial wars also shows the association of the invocation of religion and war,

> Lugal Jaggisi (2300 BC) of Babylon declared himself as the representative of God Inlil, and in the name of religion, to win over the neighbouring areas, launched a war. According to one ancient legend in the battle between Lagas and Umma tribes in Sumer, the God of Lagas tribe trapped the army of Umma tribe like birds. Around 1000 BC apart from plunder, Assyrians launched wars to establish the rule of Asur, the father of all the Gods. (Sharma 2003, 75)

Sometimes, even these clergy, the divine authorities, accompanied the warrior kings to keep the umbrella of blessing on them so that their king would be victorious over the enemy. The enemy is always wrong and my king is always right is the basic dictum. The victims of wars, apart from soldiers, are ordinary people whose crime is that they live in the enemy territory. So, on the one hand, the divine highest authority is supposed to be the protector of whole humanity, but, on the other hand, when it comes to war, the ones belonging to the other side of the divide become lesser beings and deserve to be killed and plundered. The plight of women in these wars is beyond words: anyway, they are regarded as the property of the men, and so if they are the property of the enemy, it is just like crushing the flower garden owned by the enemy and nothing more. And the clergy on both sides are always there to uphold the rightness of their own king.

If the battles happen to be between the kings of two sects within a single religion, the logic offered is different. If the kings belong to two different religions, the language is different. The new dimension which has been added in recent times is that even the reaction to such goals has been articulated in the language of religion at times.

Hinduism: *Dharmayudha*

Dharma as we have seen has two meanings. One pertains to religious moral duty. Since Hinduism is riddled with caste hierarchy and gender hierarchy, the religious duties are different for different sets of social subsets, *kshatriyas* (kings, governors, warriors, and soldiers), *vaishyas* (cattle herders, agriculturists, businessmen, artisans, and merchants), *shudras* (laborers and service providers), and women. The second meaning pertains to the religious institution, the clergy. In Hinduism, the clergy is very scattered and the sects are too many to be recounted. The major clerical organization came up in the form of Shankaracharya in eighth century. Prior to this, kings had their *rajgurus* (royal counselors), some of whom accompanied them even in the battlefields to provide the umbrella of their blessings. *Dharma* has been put sometimes as the motive, and sometimes as a provider of moral values in acts of violence and aggression.

There are numerous mentions about the wars in the holy books such as Mahabharat and Ramayana. There are mentions of wars between *sur* (God) and *asur* (devils). As such, these were the wars between the Aryans and the natives. Around these times, Aryans started worshipping gods of war for their victory and for the defeat of the natives, the non-Aryans. These battles also came to be declared as the ones between *dharma* (*surs*, Aryans) and *adharma* (*asurs*, natives).

This association between *dharma* and war came to be touted as *dharmayudha*, or holy war. In the Gita, the holy book of Hindus, Lord Krishna advises Arjun, the warrior, on one side of the battlefield, reluctant to take up arms against his close relatives who happened to be on the other side of the divide, "If you get killed in the war, you will go to heaven, and if you win, you will have the pleasure of ruling this world. Only if you fight without any feeling of profit or loss will you be saved from the sin."

The Mahabharat repeatedly mentions the reincarnation of God coming to the earth to defeat the asurs, and in this the use of deceit is also sanctioned as a religious duty. In Ramayana, Ram's battle is supposed to be sanctioned by dharma, and victory of Ram over Ravan is the victory of dharma over adharma. There is an open incitement for violence against nonbelievers, atheists, those who deny the authority of Vedas: Sukta 18–18 of Mandala 7 states, "Oh Indra! Many of your enemies have been won over by you. The active atheists need to be controlled. Atheists damage your worshippers, to oppose them send the powerful warriors to kill them."

Many ceremonies which were associated with power were also performed as the religious ones due to the close alliance between kings and the clergy. The ceremony to establish the status of the chief was gradually made more elaborate and took the form of a religious event, the Rajsuya Yagya.

> Once the chief had been initiated and his legal status established, he was eligible to perform the year long rajsuya or consecration, investing him with divinity brought from the gods by the magic power of the priests. The ritual involved rites of purification and rebirth.... After some years the consecration ceremony was followed by sacrifices, intended to assist his rejuvenation. (Thapar 2002, 121)

Ashavamedh, the horse sacrifice, was another such ceremony blessed by the priests where the king could expand his area of influence, his kingdom.

> After due ceremonies, a raja released a special horse to wander at will, accompanied by substantial bodyguard. The raja claimed the territory over which it wandered. The sacrifice was theoretically permitted to only those who were powerful and could support such a claim, but in effect it was to become ritual of kingship.... These sacrifices were conducted on a vast scale, with many priests and sacrificial animals, and a variety of objects used in the ceremony.... Such rituals reinforced the special status of raja and the Brahman.

Christianity: Crusades

The followers of Christianity were persecuted by the State till the third century when Emperor Constantine adopted this religion. After this, Christianity got the State recognition and the rulers used this legitimacy for the repression of dissidents. This repression was in the name of Christianity with the Church throwing its might with the State. Roman Emperor Theodosius (AD 379–395) declared Christianity as the State religion. On his instructions, the non-Christian institutions were banned and banished. With institutionalization and State recognition, the Church aligned with State power and became an accomplice in the policies of the State. The dissenters were harassed and punished.

Kings' expansionist goals used the cover of Christianity to get control of Jerusalem. This city is regarded as sacred, holy land by Jews, Christians, and Muslims. Using these sentiments, many kings launched their wars to take control of this city. Between 1096 and 1272, eight crusades were launched by Christian kings, mostly in alliance with the Church, to take control of this city, and in the process thousands lost their lives. Crusade as such means holy war, a war unleashed with the sanction of the Pope against nonbelievers.

> The rulers of Western Europe launched wars to take control of Holy land of Palestine between 1096 to 1291, termed as crusades. While the background of this war was blind faith, the wars were also motivated by the desire to control more land and also with commercial motives. (Sharma 2003, 96)

There were military expeditions to capture the 'holy land', Jerusalem. The Christians were aroused in the name of religion to participate in the war. These efforts were part of a large effort by European kings to increase their area of influence. Arab kings, of Islamic faith, had conquered the area of the Mediterranean seas and Jerusalem. Most of the Arab rulers permitted Christian pilgrims to visit these places. When Turkish kings won this area, they created problems for the Christian pilgrims. By this time, the Church had become powerful and had its own vested interests. In the early 1090s, Byzantine emperor Alexius Comnenus asked Pope Urban for help. Urban saw this as an opportunity to expand the influence of the Church. He urged the European knight to stop their fights and win over the holy land after the meeting known as the Council of Clermont. The battle was launched with the slogan, 'God wills it'. This slogan acted as a great mobilizer of the people, who laid down their lives in the forthcoming invasion. This was a complex offensive in which different participants had different motives, the kings wanted to expand their kingdoms, Church its hold and profit, Normans hoped to win glory, and merchants hoped to get new markets.

> Feudal lords who took part in the crusades made no secret of their intention of plundering the economically developed among the countries of the east and to seize new lands and serfs. The cities of northern Italy— Genoa, Venice, and Pisa—which played a large part in organizing the crusades, counted on being able to restore direct links with eastern shores of Mediterranean, after seizing Syria and Palestine from Seljuks and then to drive out their rivals, the Byzantine empire, from the sphere of eastern trade. (Judelson 1989, 139)

The backbone of the crusading armies was provided by the younger sons of knights and feudal lords who did not expect much land in inheritance.

The crusades consolidated and extended the influence of the Roman Catholic Church, which also fanned religious fanaticism and brought about the subordination of Orthodox Churches in Rome. The serfs who participated were looking for gaining freedom and new lands.

> At that time discontent was rife amongst peasant who found it difficult to reconcile themselves to exorbitant obligations demanded of them. There was succession of bad harvests in the years 1095–1097 and the peasants were reduced to eating grass…. Many peasants left lands to which they were bound in search of less burdensome existence. (Manfred 1974, 200)

These led to the formation of crusader states, which lasted up to the end of the 13th century. It is not only that the crusades were launched in the name of freeing Jerusalem. In the 13th century, Germans launched a crusade against the Slavonic and other people from the Baltic lands. Crusades also provided cover to the papacy to organize punitive expeditions to root out heresies.

The overview of the details of these expeditions shows that religion was not the motive, but just a convenient pretext. Pope Urban, in 1095, while giving the call for the first crusade, promised all those participating the absolution from sins and also rich booty as a reward.

> After a long and difficult journey this force finally reached Jerusalem in 1099. They took the city by storm and then instigated a brutal massacre of Muslim population. A number of crusader states were set up in Syrian and Palestinian territory. They were ruled by European nobles who ruled by a complex and strict hierarchy of lesser lords and knights. The European peasants, just like their local counterparts, found themselves in economic bondage and had thus achieved no easing of their lot. (Manfred 1974, 200)

It is noteworthy that during the fourth crusade, the knights plundered Constantinople, a Christian city (1204), making it clear that their goal was plunder and not religion, whatever that meant for them.

How the name of religion can incite emotions which are dangerous for the society becomes clear when one notes the Children's Crusade (1202). These children were stirred by religious emotions to go to the holy land. There were two such armies, one from France and another from Germany. Most of the children died on their way due to hunger and cold, some drowned in the sea, and none of them reached the destined holy land.

Islam: Jihad

Of all the religions which are supposed to be associated with violence, Islam is regarded as the most violent one. The rise of Islam has been amidst the period of wars and turmoil. Because of this, various ideas about war, war for the community, etc. are a part of the literature of the religion. On the one hand, its lopsided interpretation has been projected to prove its violent nature, and on the other, various Muslim rulers have misused the word *jihad* for their material goals of expansion of their territories and their kingdoms.

To begin with, Prophet Muhammad preached the message of his religion amidst a violent milieu. Karen Armstrong, one of the renowned scholars of Islam, pointed out,

> Islam has been dubbed as the religion of the sword, a faith which has abandoned true spirituality by sanctifying violence and intolerance. It is

an image that has dogged Islam in the Christian West ever since Middle Ages, even though Christians were fighting their own holy wars (crusade) in the middle-east at that time.... Unlike Jesus, however, Muhammad did not have the luxury of being born 'when all the world was at peace'. He was born into the bloodbath of seventh century Arabia where the old values were being radically undermined and nothing adequate had yet appeared to take their place.... Muhammad had arrived at Medina in September 622 as a refugee who had narrowly escaped death. He would continue to be in mortal danger for next five years, and during this time the *umma* (the community) faced the possibility of extermination. In the West we often imagine Muhammad as a warlord, brandishing his sword in order to impose Islam on a reluctant world by force of arms. The reality was quite different. Muhammad and first Muslims were fighting for their lives and they had also undertaken a project in which violence was inevitable. (Armstrong 2001, 165–68)

Initial appeals for *jihad* served to consolidate the political and religious unity of Arabs. "The spirit of Jihad entered Islam at Badr. It is the spirit that inspires amongst its believers a heroism beyond bounds of reason; equally it inspires dread among those outside the fold of Allah. Its root lies in Arabic jahd, meaning exertion or striving" (Akbar 2002, 24). The conceptual *jihad* is of various types, of which the one resorting to arms comes lower on the scale of importance. Yusuf Ibish (Beirut academic) wrote,

The greater Jihad is fighting one's animal tendencies. It is internal rather than external; striving in the path of God to overcome one's animal side. Man shares with animals certain characteristics, which if let loose make him a very dangerous beast. To bring these passions under control that is what Jihad means.... The lesser Jihad-fighting on behalf of community, in its defense, is a duty incumbent on Muslim provided he is attacked. (Noorani 2002, 36–37)

Historically, the word *jihad* was used rhetorically by the imperialist powers to justify their worldly expansionist designs. In its original sense, *jihad* was more of an inner moral cleansing for the community. This was called Jihad-e-Akbar (The Great Jihad). But now, the whole notion of *jihad* is being used as an instrument for legitimizing militaristic, monarchic, and dictatorial regimes. As for these radical Islamist groups, *jihad* is being used as a cynical ruse to whip up religious fervor for their cause (Mushirul Hasan, Interview, Tehelka.com; http://englishmatters. gmu.edu/issue6/911exhibit/emails/demystifyingtheislamicogre.htm [last accessed on August 28, 2014]).

> As per the tents of Islam, *jihad* is not one of the pillars of Islam, …it remains a duty for Muslims to commit themselves to a struggle on all fronts—moral, spiritual and political—to create a just and decent society, where the poor and vulnerable are not exploited, in the way that God had intended men to live. Fighting and warfare might sometimes be necessary, but it was only a minor part of the whole Jihad or struggle. (Noorani 2002, 38)

Similarly, Asghar Ali Engineer, a scholar of Islam, points out,

> It is Jihad, which is one of the pillars of Islam precisely because it does not necessarily mean war. Jihad…means utmost effort, not violence and it is obligatory on Muslims to make utmost efforts (in wisely manner) to spread the message of Allah so as to create a just and compassionate society. This is what is obligatory, not waging a war at all. Prophet himself has exemplified it on many occasions especially at the time of Slh-I-Hudabiya (i.e. peace of Hudaibiyah and Fath-I-Mecca). (Engineer 1998)

Since there is an original mention of *jihad* in the literature related to Prophet Muhammad, it has come to be identified with Islam in a deeper way. But the real meaning and its misuse by Muslim kings and others also gets tagged to Islam more so than in other religions. The context of the rise of Islam got associated with the rule of later kings' behavior.

The attack of Muhammad bin Qasim on Sindh in the year 712–713 also was backed by the emotional incitement from Islam, while it was purely Qasim's attempt to expand the area of his operation. Similarly, Mahmud Ghazni's plundering of Somnath temple is also associated with Islam, while on his way to Somnath, Ghazni had also had a battle with Abdul Fath Daud. Mahmud also had plans to attack the Islamic Caliph of Basra. Many Muslim kings, either Shia against Sunni or even amongst the same sect, had been fighting, sometimes deriving legitimacy from religion as well. The seven-year-long battle between Iraq and Iran was called *jihad* by Ayatollah Khoemini, and his rival Saddam, another Muslim, was vanquished by the United States under the flag of self-protection from the terrorist Islamic state.

The third crusade launched by the Christian rulers was fought back by Saladin, a Muslim General. Interestingly, he not only conquered Jerusalem but also went on to win over Egypt and Syria. Saladin was called the hero of Islam, while he battled not only against the crusading Christian armies but also against the Muslim rulers of Egypt and Syria.

Currently, the acts of Taliban and Al Qaeda have also been labeled as *jihad*. We have seen in detail in earlier chapters how Taliban and Al Qaeda were actively promoted by the US policies in the Middle East to take control of Afghanistan. The training of Al Qaeda, the very coining of the term *jihad* for their anti-Soviet actions, is to be seen in the light of current political contingencies of imperialism. In the post-Vietnam era, the United States was reluctant to send its armies to have Afghanistan evacuated by Soviet forces and then occupy it. The United States had its strategic interests of control on the oil resources in mind. It operated through its minion Pakistan to get youths trained as terrorists and called their endeavor *jihad*. It worked well. It not only resulted in the occupation of Afghanistan by the United States in due course, but also succeeded in demonizing Islam, which was to provide the pretext for attacking Muslim countries like Iraq in due course.

Appendices

Appendix A: How Not to Investigate and Punish a Crime—The Case of Afzal Guru

The death penalty given by the Supreme Court to hang Muhammad Afzal Guru on October 20, 2006 was deferred by the President of India. There were two sets of petitions lying on the President's table, one demanding his immediate hanging and the other asking for clemency and reduction of his punishment to a life sentence. Guru was one of the accused in the case of assault on the Parliament on December 13, 2001, in which eight security personnel and one gardener were killed. Guru was not found to be part of any terrorist outfit, nor did he play any direct role in the same. In the trial which took place, the provisions of the International Covenant on Civil and Political Rights had not been respected. The Supreme Court noted that there was no direct evidence of his involvement. The evidence was mainly circumstantial. All three courts, including the Supreme Court, acquitted him of the charges under the POTA of belonging to either a terrorist organization or a terrorist group. The courts also noted that the evidence was fabricated. Most importantly, he was not given any worthwhile legal assistance to defend him during interrogation.

When Ram Jethmalani offered to be the lawyer for Geelani, Hindutva goons attacked his office. One also recalls here that the lawyers offering to hold the brief of those accused in the July 11, 2006, Mumbai blasts were also threatened by the Hindutva outfit, a real case of cowardly display of pseudo-patriotism. At best, Guru was a facilitator in the crime and not a direct perpetrator of the crime; the evidence against him was merely circumstantial and that the police lied about the time and place of arrest, fabricated evidence including arrest memos, and extracted false confessions. The court noted that he was not a member of any banned organization.

The conviction under Section 3(2) of POTA is set aside. The conviction under Section 3(5) of POTA is also set aside because there is no evidence that he is a member of a terrorist organization, once the confessional statement is excluded. Incidentally, we may mention that even going by confessional statement, it is doubtful whether the membership of a terrorist gang or organization is established.

Further, it was said, "The incident, which resulted in heavy casualties, had shaken the entire nation and the collective conscience of the society will only be satisfied if capital punishment is awarded to the offender." So does that mean that the punishment was being given to assuage the collective national conscience? One must add that what is presented as this conscience is the consciousness of a section of the dominant middle classes.

Many a human rights activist of repute sat on a *dharana* (protest demonstration) demanding the commutation of the death sentence to life imprisonment. They issued appeals to the same effect and also floated petitions for clemency. Not to be left behind, another section of activists floated counterpetitions demanding nothing short of death penalty for this 'terrorist'. In various talk shows, the angry audience hooted down those talking of the facts of the case and asking for leniency in the light of the holes in the story built by the police authorities. There are two major questions involved in the case: (1) Should death penalty be given in the rarest of rare cases?; (2) When world over the brutal capital punishment is being done away with, should we stick to it? The other peripheral issues which are trying to undermine the basic issues are the hysterical nationalism of the Hindu right and sections of society who do not think that the crimes of those accused of acts of terror 'also' need to be proved before they are punished, and that the punishment has to be commensurate with the crime. For them, once the Supreme Court has ruled, the doors for clemency are closed.

The base on which the Supreme Court gave its judgment was built by the police with methods which are questionable, which have also been reprimanded by the court in this case. The argument on the other side was that if Guru was not hanged, it would be an insult to those who laid down their lives in defending the Parliament. And that other terrorist acts à la Kandhar may be undertaken to bargain for his release.

The other question, which has got mixed up with this, is the fate of the peace process which is going on in Kashmir and South Asia as a whole. In the visual media debates, one can see the hysterical nationalism oozing from every pore of Hindu right wing and some others. Some Muslim spokespersons of this or the other party find this the best opportunity to wear their patriotism on their sleeves by taking blinded, firm positions against any consideration of clemency. This became most obvious when Mukhtar Abbas Naqvi of BJP went to the extent of denying that Bhagat Singh's kin could ever make a clemency petition in this case, to the loud applause of the studio audience. As a matter of fact, Bhagat Singh's kin Prof. Jagmohan Singh and Anand Patwardhan, the noted documentary filmmaker and rights activist, had issued the appeal carried by the media. It is unlikely that the BJP spokesperson would have missed it; anyway, sometimes even feigned ignorance is necessary to pursue one's political assertions! The response of letter writers in the newspaper columns was no different. Most of them demanded the blood of this 'terrorist'! Nothing else can reflect the state of 'social common sense' in the society. By now, communal violence has become acceptable in the society. It is justified to the extent that those involved in it are neither punished nor even looked down upon. On the other hand, anybody remotely linked to acts of terror can be hanged without any pangs of conscience; communal patriotism at its worst is on display.

While the Supreme Court deserves all the respect, one has to see that the primary investigation done by the police, whatever its flaws, forms the base of the judgment. When that investigation has holes, should it be accepted as it is presented? When the primary culprits are either dead or absconding, can 'the whole truth be out'? Or is it that somebody has to be punished anyway to quench the thirst for revenge, and who better than the one who has a Muslim name and happens to be from Kashmir. The whole trial of Afzal needs to be looked at again; the flaws of the investigation, the weakness of and deliberate violation of norms by the police authorities, and the absence of competent legal assistance to Afzal should alert us to the fact that something is seriously amiss in the whole story. The worst fallout of the hanging of Afzal is that the real truth will remain buried due to the shoddy investigation and the real culprits may not be apprehended at all, whosoever they are.

Merely being guided by Islamophobia is no guarantee for the correctness of the story of prosecution. Afzal's letters and the appeal of his wife, which have been ignored, have a lot to tell. Even the role of the media in pushing Afzal to the hangman's noose should be looked at carefully; we need to make sure that 'trial by media' does not become the base of our legal system. The quality of judgments is the backbone of the strength of democracy. The State is all-powerful and holds the authority to hang someone on shoddy grounds, but at the same time it will be hanging the very concept of a 'just' legal system. Let us have a look at the vulnerability of Afzal Guru, a Kashmiri, a poor man, and an ex-militant not being able to afford legal cover; is that not ground enough to relook at the case? Even the verdict of the apex court, that presidential pardon is subject to review by the same system which has given punishment, nullifies the very basic of the provision of presidential pardon. It needs to be debated whether the President has this power or whether from now on there will be no appeal once the apex court has given its verdict even if that is based on an investigation full of gaping holes.

Kashmir has been reduced to 'our' real estate, where we are posting millions of our soldiers to deal with a couple of thousands of militants! Surely, if there is one Indian soldier for every seventh Kashmiri, no wonder Kashmiris will see it as an occupation army. Having said that, the punishment meted out to Guru is not commensurate with the crime committed by him; one will also endorse that the very notion of capital punishment is nothing but barbarism, and it does not become dignified if it is given to a suspected terrorist. Many of those otherwise swearing by nonviolence are so communalized at the core that they are at the forefront of some or the other move demanding the hanging of Guru.

One can understand that for RSS and its affiliates this is the golden opportunity to display their patriotism, partly also to wash the sin of accompanying the terrorists to Kandhar by one of their ministers. One can also understand the success of RSS in communalizing the social thinking to the extent that now truth and humane values have ceased to matter in the face of communal thinking. Justice is being converted into revenge and punishment is meant to further communalize the society rather than be a means of reform, and an occasion to introspect as to why such crimes are going on. Surely, no one is born a terrorist and no one likes to resort to these means by choice. The deeper circumstances under which these acts of violence are taking place need to be given a thought. One understands that terrorism is a mere symptom of the underlying disease, which has roots in injustices somewhere. One also understands that terrorism cannot be eradicated by killing the terrorists. For that, the underlying causes have to be addressed.

The double standards of our society and legal system are becoming glaringly apparent. The perpetrators of communal violence not only get away with their crimes but also sometimes get promotions, as in the case of Ramdeo Tyagi of Maharashtra, the one who led the attack on Suleiman Bakery in Mumbai during the 1992–1993 riots. Hundreds of police officials who have been named in the inquiry commission reports are enjoying the 'fruits' of their crimes of omission and commission. Thackeray and Modi, who have been the main architects of the Mumbai and Gujarat riots, respectively, could not even be touched by the long arm of law. On the contrary, they landed up increasing their political clout after presiding over these genocides. While the perpetrators of the Mumbai riots are having a gala time, the culprits of subsequent bomb blasts are being meted out the punishments due to them. The general impression is gaining ground in the society that by now there are two legal systems in the society. One for the followers of Hindu communalism, like the killer of Pastor Stains, Dara Singh, who was spared the noose and hailed as a *Hindu dharma rakshak* (protector of Hindu faith), where the perpetrators of communal violence get away with ease. The other one is for those who belong to minorities. In their case, even the remotest association with the terror attacks is ground enough for hanging or the severest possible punishment.

In Kashmir, the Indian army is seen as the occupation army, which has tortured thousands of innocents; Chittisingpura is just the tip of iceberg. The hanging of Maqbool Butt in 1984 did give a feeling of alienation and later a boost to militancy. Who do we blame for that? Those calling for a hangman for Guru surely were bent upon repeating the process. True Nation can hang those who have not committed the crime of grave severity. What is to be kept in mind is that due to such punishments very adverse processes may come to the fore. So, there is a need to overcome communal myopia. We must distinguish between the hysterical nationalism of the likes of those demanding the hanging and the humane nationalism calling for reconsideration of the punishment meted out, to quench the feverish pitch of communalized sections of society. This hanging may reinforce the perception, which is already prevalent, that there are two sets of legal norms prevalent in the country.

Appendix B: In the Name of SIMI

In the third week of July 2009, the Maharashtra police arrested several Muslims in Pusad, Akola, and neighboring regions on the charge that they were reviving SIMI under a new name. It was after a fairly long time that one had heard of arrests in the name of SIMI. The earlier cycle of arrest of Muslim youths, which was a matter of routine after every blast, such as in the cases of Malegaon, Mecca Masjid in Hyderabad, Jaipur, and other places, was broken with the impeccable proof of Sadhvi Pragya Singh Thakur's motorcycle being found in Malegaon. The motorcycle link led to Swami Dayanand Pandey, Lt. Col. Shrikant Purohit, and many others associated with Hindu right-wing organizations, offshoots of or inspired by RSS ideology.

Society witnessed that after most of the blasts, Muslim youths were arrested recklessly on the charge of being behind the blasts. They were harassed for months, and then released as there was no evidence. This was more or less a routine pattern and it frightened the whole Muslim community. Careers of many Muslim youths' were crushed due to these baseless arrests. Many minority families underwent severe problems and as they were ostracized from their own community once they were dragged into the jails on the charges which were guided more by the prevalent biases or stereotypes rather than any substance. SIMI came to be regarded as the core organization responsible for fomenting trouble through youth. Despite the ban on SIMI in 2001, the Muslim youth kept on being labeled as SIMI activists and were put behind the bar.

It is not to say that SIMI was upholding an ideology which talked of democracy and secularism. One knows that SIMI, which began as a student front of Jamat-e-Islami Hind, gradually came out of its control and became radical in the 1990s in particular. Yoginder Sikand, an Islamic scholar of repute, gives a very crisp history of this organization (www.countercurrents.org/comm-sikand150706.htm [last accessed on October 10, 2014]). SIMI was founded on the ideology propounded by

Maulana Maududi, according to whom all non-Muslims are *kafirs*, man-made systems such as democracy are false and sharia is the only correct way. It aimed at spreading Islamic consciousness amongst Muslim students and peaceful missionary work amongst non-Muslims. Some events in the decade of 1990 were to shape its ideology in a radical and militant direction. These events were Soviet Russia's invasion of Afghanistan and Islamization of Pakistan in particular.

Meanwhile, Jamat-e-Islami came to accept democracy and secularism as its guiding ideology. SIMI came out from the control of its parent organization to talk in a different language. The demolition of the Babri Masjid and the post-demolition violence gave it a fillip in the negative direction. It said that democracy had failed to protect Muslims so there was a need for someone like Mohammed Ghazni, the destroyer of Somnath. This was also the theme of the poster released by them in the aftermath of the Babri demolition. It was alleged that SIMI had links with Sikh and Kashmiri militants, and with Osama and the ISI. At the same time that SIMI claimed that it wanted to work through peaceful methods, the worsening communal situation made to say that Muslims are a belabored community. Under these circumstances, SIMI was banned in 2001.

The ban on SIMI was challenged. A tribunal was set up to review the ban. Ajit Sahi of *Tehelka* in his painstaking investigation followed the tribunal's sitting all through (*Tehelka*, SIMI Fictions, August 12, 2008; http://archive.tehelka.com/story_main40.asp?filename=Ne160808thekafka_project.asp [last accessed on August 28, 2014]). The tribunal did not find any evidence of the charges put against SIMI for banning it. The ban could not be upheld. About this investigation, Ajit Sahi said, "…his investigation is no dry story rising from lifeless court documents. It has been an emotional roller coaster to sit across young boys barely into manhood, their foreheads creased by sleepless nights worried stiff over the jailing of a father, a brother, wondering endlessly," 'Will this end? Is this for real? What do I do now? Where do I go now? Will I survive this?'. He further says, "…as I interviewed countless Muslims, so weathered, I couldn't but ask myself, What if this was me? What if it was my brother, my father in jail?"

With the world scenario tilting against Islam and Muslims due to, radical Islamists trained in the madrassas set up in Pakistan with the US aid, the popular psyche perceived an average Muslim as a terrorist and police machinery operated on this understanding. Even when scores of lives were shattered and the community came under the intimidation of highest order, the government did not put any correctives to this pattern of investigation.

Disturbed by this situation, two people's tribunals were set up by human rights groups. The reports and recommendations of both the tribunals are similar and overlapping. The first one was headed by Justices (Retd.) Bhargava and Sardar Ali Khan, with prominent social activists like Asghar Ali Engineer and Prashant Bhushan in the jury. The testimonies showed that a large number of innocent young Muslims have been and are being victimized by the police on the charge of being involved in various terrorist acts across the country. This is particularly so in Maharashtra, Gujarat, Madhya Pradesh, Andhra Pradesh, and Rajasthan, though not limited to these states. This victimization and demonization of Muslims in the guise of investigation of terror offences is having a very serious psychological impact on the minds of not only the families of the victims but also other members of the community. It is leading to a very strong sense of insecurity and alienation which may lead to frightful consequences for the nation.

The second tribunal set up by different sets of organizations of Rajasthan worked under the leadership of Justice (Retd.) Bhargava. One of its pertinent observations was that the police authorities investigating the terror offences appear to be violating all the laws of the land and directions of the Supreme Court during the conduct of the investigations. In particular, many persons have been detained for days or weeks, without showing them as being arrested and without producing them before any magistrate. They have been sometimes tortured and humiliated by the police officers. They have not been allowed to meet their relatives and lawyers, who have often not even been informed of their detention. The investigation of the blasts by the police also appears to be communally motivated and only persons belonging to the Muslim community have been the target of the investigations.

The names of HUJI and SIMI have been bandied about by the police as the perpetrators of the blasts without any evidence. A number of former members of SIMI have been arrested and detained without any basis or evidence against them. The media has also been uncritically repeating and amplifying the baseless allegations and innuendoes of the police mentioning persons and organizations belonging to the Muslim community, thus, resulting in ethnic profiling and feeding into the Islamophobia being created and reinforced in the minds of the Hindu community by the Hindutva organizations. In Jaipur, this has resulted in the vilification of the entire Bengali Muslim community who has been victimized by the Hindutva organizations in complicity with the police.

Thousands of them have been picked up after the blasts and forcibly transported to New Jalpaiguri and then Bangladesh without any due process of law and without giving them an opportunity to show their Indian citizenship. This has resulted in the ethnic cleansing of Jaipur.

One does not know with what seriousness the administration looks at these people's tribunals; the fact is that they have put forward profound realities of the society. It is imperative that the government takes a serious look at these reports and instructs the investigation authorities to be more professional in their approach and sheds its biases while dealing with the minority community (http://archive.tehelka.com/story_ main40.asp?filename=Ne160808thekafka_project.asp [last accessed on October 10, 2014]).

Appendix C: The Vicious Cycle of Islamophobia

We are going through strange times. While the science, technology, and rationalism have given us physical and intellectual tools to better the lot of humanity, we are witnessing the production of provocative material, literature, and films, in particular, which demonize the particular religion, to be precise, Islam and the prophet of Islam. On the other hand, there is a section of the community that feels threatened and insecure coming to the streets to protest against such humiliation and insult of their religion. There are debates on freedom of expression, but how come the freedom of expression always goes on to humiliate and demonize one particular religion only?

In September 2012, there were massive protests in different countries against the American embassies, resulting in the death of four members of the US staff, including Ambassador Chris Stevens, in Benghazi. Different countries asked Google, the owner of YouTube, which was broadcasting a provocative and insulting video clip, 'Innocence of Muslims', to withdraw the film clip. In some places, the video clip was withdrawn and blocked. The United States stuck to its 'freedom of expression' stance and many protesters could still be seen on the streets.

The 14-minute film clip is part of the full-length feature film made by Nakoula Basseley, a US-based Christian. The film is a crude film made in extremely poor taste and is very insulting to Islam. In this film, a large modern-day mob of bearded Muslims is shown to be attacking Christians. It also takes the audience back in time to show a distorted life of Prophet Muhammad with negative and aggressive traits of personality. The film generated a strong reaction amongst a large section of Muslims. It must be pointed out that this is not the only type of reaction to this film. Sections of clerics asked Muslims to restrain from violent protests. Quoting the moral precepts of Islam from the Quran, they said that Islam is a religion of peace and no violent protests should be held. The best response to this despicable film was from a section of Muslims who distributed copies of the book on the life of Prophet Muhammad, the prophet of peace.

During the last several years, it has become a sort of standard practice by many in the West and some in India to demonize Islam. We remember the Danish cartoon of the Prophet, where he is shown as a terrorist, with a bomb tucked in his turban. A Florida pastor went on to burn the holy book, Koran, saying that Koran teaches violence. Some US soldiers in Afghanistan also burnt copies of the Koran, on the grounds that terrorist elements had written messages in those copies.

The demonization of Islam and Muslims has a pattern and agenda. The cartoons and films are the outcome of the deeper political processes, which aim to control the oil wells in West Asia. The imperialist greed of the United States marshaled the flag of 'Islam the new threat' since Ayatollah Khomeini came to power in Iran, overthrowing the US stooge Raza Shah Pahlavi. Later, the slogan was worsened with the United States setting up madrassas in Pakistan to train Al Qaeda–Taliban to initiate the Muslim youth to fight against the occupying Russian armies in Afghanistan. The words *jihad* and *kafir* were distorted to indoctrinate the Muslim youth in these madrassas. With later trajectories and the 9/11, WTC attack, the US media with all its guile popularized the phrase

'Islamic terrorism'. The phrase was picked up by the media all over the world and later became part of the social common sense. This is a major abuse of religion for political goals by the imperialist power. One can understand this demonization of Islam as a part of the US policy, a cover to hide its agenda to control the oil resources. To understand it in the terms of Noam Chomsky's phrase 'manufacturing consent', the coining of the phrase 'Islamic terrorism' is part of the US mechanism of manufacturing consent of the world to give assent to the US attacks on Afghanistan and Iraq.

This US policy has given rise to twin processes. One process is the phenomena, like Florida pastor Terry Jones burning the Koran or a Danish cartoonist drawing Prophet Muhammad as a terrorist or the aforementioned film, which have been the outcome of the intense propaganda against Islam. This US propaganda has been backed by the US-sponsored ideology of the 'clash of civilizations', according to which the current era of World History is the era of assault of the backward Islamic civilization on the advanced Western civilization. This distorted perception, resulting from 'the clash of civilizations' theory, was used as a cover for the US agenda in West Asia. The other process which started was that the psyche of the global Muslim community started being affected. The perception grew that Muslims (Afghanistan and Iraq) are being attacked; they are under threat. In India, the added aspect was the rise of RSS-type politics, bringing up the Ram temple issue and inculcating hatred for Muslims. A large section of Muslims started feeling intimidated and besieged. It became easy to mobilize them around identity issues. Any section of a community which feels besieged becomes vulnerable to easy provocation and identity-based mobilization.

It is a vicious circle, the Islamophobia on the one hand and the besieged community on the other. In this scenario, the Muslim clerics who are asking for peace are the beacon lights of hope for the community. The Muslims who are distributing the books on the life of the Prophet need to be complimented. This is what the sane response from the community has to be. What about the United States, its imperialist designs, and its mighty propaganda machinery doing all the mischief in the world? Can there be a process of controlling that? Under Kofi Annan, when he was Secretary General of the UN, a high-level committee produced a report, 'Alliance of Civilizations'. This report got lost under the barrage of Islamphobia. It is time the world as such takes note of the deeper humane values which have been developed by humanity over a period of time, the values which have led to the reports of the likes of 'Alliance of Civilizations', the UN conventions which have conceptualized human rights for all.

The triggers which have incited the demonization process of religion and films like the ones mentioned above are provoking these insane reactions from a section of Muslims. Can the UN be revived as a global platform for monitoring the norms for nations, media, and other aspects of our global life evolved to ensure that democratization and human dignity is promoted? Can the world come forward to check the aggressions of 'the Superpower'? That is when such films will cease to act as factors promoting violent reactions. And even such crude attempts at insulting others' religions will reduce. Maybe, with such norms and restraints on the US policies, we can hope that such incidents will reduce. Even if there are elements making some films like this one, there will be others making films giving their own versions of the Prophet's mission of peace in the world.

And finally, we also need to preserve the concept of freedom of expression moderated with its limits. We also need to cultivate methods of protest where hysterical emotions are kept at bay and a rational approach is brought to the fore.

Appendix D: International Jury

The War Crimes Tribunal: Afghanistan

International Tribunal: War Crimes against Afghanistan (excerpts)
17. Verdict:

> I find the defendant George Walker Bush, President of the United States and Commander-in-Chief of United States Armed Forces, guilty:
>
> 1. Under Article 2 of the Statute of the International Criminal Tribunal for Afghanistan (ICTA), and under International Criminal Law, for waging a war of aggression against Afghanistan and the Afghan people.

2. Under Article 3, Part I, Clause (a), (b), (c),(d), (f),(g) and Article 3, Part II, clause (a), (b), (c), (d), (e), (f), (h), (i), (k), (l), (n), (o), (p), (q) of the Statute of the International Criminal Tribunal for Afghanistan (ICTA), under International Criminal Law and International Humanitarian Law, in respect of war crimes committed against the people of Afghanistan by the use of weapons prohibited by the laws of warfare, causing death and destruction to the Afghan people; maiming men, women, and children.

3. Under Article 4, Clause (a), (b), (d), (e), (f), (h), and (i) of the Statute of the International Criminal Tribunal and International Humanitarian Law, for crimes against humanity, committed against the people of Afghanistan, resulting in inhumane acts affecting large sections of the population caused by the military invasion, bombing, and lack of humanitarian relief.

4. Under Article 3, Part I, Clause (a), (b), (c), (f), (g) and Article 3, Part II, clause (f), (k), (p), and (q) of the Statute of the ICTA, under International Criminal Law and the Hague Convention and Geneva Convention (III) of 1949 in respect of the torture and killings of Taliban, and other prisoners of war who had surrendered, and their torture and inhumane conditions of detention and deportation of innocent civilians.

In respect of the transport of prisoners in 'sealed containers' and their death due to suffocation and firing of rifle shots at the container for creating holes for ventilation with the prisoners inside, and for conditions at Sheberghan prison, the defendant is entitled to benefit of doubt at this trial; however, the issues are left open for trial, before any other court/tribunal, as the evidence before the tribunal is not conclusive on the involvement of United States forces.

5. Under Article 3, Part I (c) and (g); Article 3, Part 2 (a), (b), (c), (d), (e), (h), (i), (l); and Article 4 (b), (l) of (n), (p), (q) of the ICTA in respect of the serious humanitarian situation resulting from the refugee exodus in Afghanistan due to the bombing of civilian population and civilian infrastructure in a country already affected by serious famine resulting in mass exodus of people and death from bombing, hunger, displacement, disease, and absence of humanitarian relief....

(http://www.mindfully.org/Reform/2004/Afghanistan-Criminal-Tribunal10mar04.htm [last accessed on August 28, 2014]).

Appendix E: International Tribunal on War Crimes Against Iraq

Statement of the Jury of Conscience
Istanbul, June 27, 2005

> "The attack on Iraq is an attack on justice, on liberty, on our safety, on our future, on us all"

With a Jury of Conscience from 10 different countries hearing the testimonies of 54 members of the Panel of Advocates who came from all across the world, including Iraq, the United States, and the United Kingdom, this global civil initiative came to an end with a press conference at the Hotel Armada where the Chair of the Jury of Conscience, Arundhati Roy, announced the Jury's conclusions.

The Jury defined this war as one of the most unjust in history:

> The Bush and Blair administrations blatantly ignored the massive opposition to the war expressed by millions of people around the world. They embarked upon one of the most unjust, immoral, and cowardly wars in history. The Anglo-American occupation of Iraq of the last 27 months has led to the destruction and devastation of the Iraqi state and society. Law and order have broken down completely, resulting in a pervasive lack of human security; the physical infrastructure is in shambles; the health care delivery system is a mess; the education system has ceased to function; there is massive environmental and ecological devastation; and the cultural and archeological heritage of the Iraqi people has been desecrated.

On the basis of the preceding findings and recalling the Charter of the United Nations and other legal documents, the Jury has established the following charges against the governments of the United States and the UK:

- Planning, preparing, and waging the supreme crime of a war of aggression in contravention of the UN Charter and the Nuremberg Principles.
- Targeting the civilian population of Iraq and civilian infrastructure.
- Using disproportionate force and indiscriminate weapon systems.

- Failing to safeguard the lives of civilians during military activities and during the occupation period thereafter.
- Using deadly violence against peaceful protestors.
- Imposing punishments without charge or trial, including collective punishment.
- Subjecting Iraqi soldiers and civilians to torture and cruel, inhuman, or degrading treatment.
- Actively creating conditions under which the status of Iraqi women has seriously been degraded.

The Jury also provided a number of recommendations that include:

> recognizing the right of the Iraqi people to resist the illegal occupation of their country and to develop independent institutions, and affirming that the right to resist the occupation is the right to wage a struggle for self-determination, freedom, and independence as derived from the Charter of the United Nations, we the Jury of Conscience declare our solidarity with the people of Iraq and the immediate and unconditional withdrawal of the coalition forces from Iraq. (Excerpts; see http://www.democraticunderground.com/discuss/duboard.php?az=view_all&address=102x1584405 [last accessed on August 28, 2014])

Appendix F: Scapegoats and Holy Cows

A tribunal was organized by 'Anhad' and associated human rights organizations in Hyderabad (2007). It had a very demanding task of hearing and finding the truth behind the allegations against the accused. The tribunal found that there has been a gross violation of laws by the police. Not only that alleged culprits were kept in custody and denied all their rights; their relatives were also not informed, and their date of arrest was shown to be much later than the real time they were picked up. The torture to which they were subjected to is beyond words; the wrecking of poor families which took place due to the whole process shattered their lives. The careers of many promising young men were totally ruined due to such arrests without any proof whatsoever. Lack of professional attitude and biases were evident in the attitude of police.

The pattern observed in most of the cases was that there were illegal detentions for long time. Following the torture if the person is to be released it seems that police follows a norm and takes the signature of the accused on a blank paper. The accused are threatened with dire consequences if they go to human rights activists or lawyers. At times they are made to shout Jai Shri Ram just to humiliate them. Sometimes even possession of Urdu literature is taken as a proof of terrorist links. Third degree torture to the accused and severe torture to the relatives of the accused to elicit confession is employed very widely. The accused and their relatives are taken to the police station or other places of detention on false pretexts and the elementary needs of water and food are not looked at. For permitting the families to see the accused under custody a bribe is extracted most of the times.

What happens to the future of those who are accused and released later? The students lose their career track; at times colleges do not take them back until court ruling is brought to that effect. The families of accused get ostracized from the community out of fear. Others stop relating to them. The business gets a severe setback and at these times banks refuse to give them loans, etc. Some of the accused are also tempted to become approvers with the carrot dangled in front of them that they will be released. The powers vested with the police seem to be present only through there misuse, most of the times.

A two-way impression operates in the society. First, the larger sections of society feel that Muslim terrorists are a big threat to the nation. Second, amongst Muslims, the feeling is that state is totally partisan and deliberate injustice is being done to them since they are Muslims. Two sets of mechanisms of investigation norms are coming to be rooted. First, Muslim youth are picked up after every blast and are subjected to torture till courts pronounce them non-guilty. Second, the blasts accused who are Hindus are treated with kid gloves.

(No)Crime and Punishment

The state of crime and punishment is very paradoxical in current times. Those guilty of communal violence generally get away without any punishment, while the innocents are being punished in acts of terror, just because they happen to belong to a particular religion. In the current scenario, the current policing and social system seems to operate on the assumption that Muslims are terrorists. Both communal violence and war against terror have demonized and targeted them in particular. While the society at large has come to believe in various myths about minorities, a large section of the police force has acted in the most prejudicial and biased manner on the issues related to violence in the name of religion and in the case of terrorist violence.

There have been innumerable cases of Muslim youth being picked up in the aftermath of terror attacks, incarcerated in jails, and then let off as the legal protective mechanisms, though painfully slow, catch up to intervene and release some of these accused. While every such case of a young man is a heartrending tale, and every such case of police action ruins the family and career of the accused, the one related to Muhammad Aamir Khan aged 32 (in March 2012) probably ranks amongst the most horrendous ones. The other interesting aspect of this young man trying to restart his life all over again is that he is full of appreciation of the positive aspects of the system and acknowledges the good aspects of the system, which released him from dark dungeons after 14 long and tortuous years. The same system mercifully kept him connected to the outside world, the interlude in solitary confinement notwithstanding.

Aamir, a 10th standard student, aged 18, was abducted by the Delhi police and charged of being the mastermind of acts of terror and other related crimes. The methods employed by the police need not be recounted, as while the talk of police reforms, etc. is there 'on paper', the brutality of the many men in khaki uniforms continues unabated. They also keep innovating newer and newer forms of torture. The illegal act of taking signatures on blank paper seems to be routine with the 'guardians of law'. Those supposed to be protecting our law must be probably the biggest violators of law in the power dens where they are rarely answerable and generally get away with the most serious cruelties committed in the confines of their fiefdom, the police stations and jails. Aamir underwent all this. He tried to continue his study while in jail, through the IGNOU center. But that was not to last long as one police officer in his zeal of punishing the lad belonging to the 'wrong' religion put him in solitary confinement and cut off his education which he was seriously pursuing. With 14 long years in the jail, how he maintained his sanity to look forward to the study of journalism or law must be amongst some of the mysteries which our society provides in abundance.

Coming back to Aamir, while in prison, he lost his father, and his mother suffered a paralytic stroke. His family property had to be sold off to fight the infinite cases put against him by the police. The 'leaders of the community' did not have time to take up his case, and the label of 'terrorist' and that too a Pakistani one warded off many other friends and relatives from coming to help.

Today, out of jail, with two cases still hanging on his head, he is working with an NGO to make a living, taking care of his mother's expensive treatment, and trying to look forward to a life where he can become a professional of some sort. Who is responsible for the wreckage of the life of Aamir and those of the likes of him? While one can see the role of our biased police system, which regards Muslim as criminals and terrorists in the main, one can also see the role of the prevalence of biases and misconceptions about the community floating all around, duly promoted and deepened by the communal forces, our educational books, and the slant of media reporting. Now what is the responsibility of the community and the State in rehabilitating these young boys? In the Mecca Masjid blast, the accused, after being arrested, were let off and given compensation of ₹3 lakhs each. Interestingly, when they were arrested, there were banner headlines of Muslims being arrested for the blast, but when they were absolved of the charges against them, small hidden news items were all that welcomed them.

The situation during the last couple of years seems to have improved slightly, especially after Hemant Karkare's pathbreaking investigation in the Malegaon blast, the Rajasthan ATS taking the issue forward, and the whole saffron gang of Sadhvi Pragya Singh Thakur, Dayanand Pandey, Swami Aseemanand, and company coming under the scanner. Interestingly, once this gang was apprehended, the acts of terror also reduced substantially. The right inference needs to be drawn here. It seems that the major flaw of these investigations has been the prejudiced mind of the investigating authorities. While proper rehabilitation and suitable compensation to these youth are imperative, there is a dire need for police reforms and their torture techniques to be questioned. The rights of the prison inmates and accused need to be honored. Police authorities are reckless when it comes to Muslim youth, and those offi-cers violating the basic norms generally get away without any punish-ment. The khaki uniform seems to be giving them too much unrestrained power to wreck the lives of innocent youth. Is it not time that the case of Aamir and his likes act as a sort of mirror to our policing system? It calls for an urgent need for putting the issues related to communal harmony, the falsity of prevalent myths on high priority. Hope such introspection is one amongst those vested with lot of powers.

It is rare that an 18-year-old, after being tortured for 14 years for belonging to a particular religion, will come out with such positive senti-ments; the system also needs to introspect in the context of this young man, help him out in toto, and ensure that such acts of brutality are not repeated by the system and by men in khaki uniforms in particular.

Fabricated Cases and the State

A forum, Rihai Manch, has been formed for getting justice for youths who have been falsely implicated in acts of terror. They organized a pro-test sit-in to get justice for these youths with the implementation of the Nimesh Commission (which has gone into the cases of acts of terror and recommended the steps for justice). This forum has also demanded the arrest of the police and IB officials responsible for the death of Maulana Khalid Mujahid, the implementation of the R.D. Nimesh Commission report, and the release of innocent Muslim youths implicated in acts of terror. This campaign is getting broader support from more human rights groups and the affected community. This is a major effort by a civic society group and to democratically protest against the insensitive and biased state machinery, to pressurize it to come on the path of justice.

The Samajwadi Party, Akhilesh Yadav government in Uttar Pradesh (UP), had earlier claimed to be the major champion of the cause of Muslims, to the extent that the leader of this party, Mulayam Singh Yadav, was derogatorily called Mulla Mulayam. But during his regime also, when he came to power the last time, many episodes of communal violence took place under the very nose of the government. Currently also, Akhilesh Yadav's regime is marked by over 27 episodes of major riots. On top of that, this government in its election promise had said that the innocents implicated in the acts of terror would be released. On the contrary, the death of Maulana Khalid Mujahid in police custody raised sufficient doubts about the intentions of the government. Even the R.D. Nimesh Commission report was kept in the cold storage, and now when it has been released finally, the government is refraining from taking action, hiding behind the argument that it will be discussed in a future Assembly session before action is taken on the report. As such, the government has full prerogative to take action at the Cabinet level. People fear that this commission report may also face the same fate as the other commission reports, which are generally put on the backburner or in the cold storage.

Ashish Khaitan, one of the journalists with dogged determination, sensitivity, and honesty, has floated a portal, *Gulail* (slingshot), to highlight the investigative reports related to the framing of innocents by authorities. Many officers have falsely implicated innocents, despite knowing the truth, to enhance their own career prospects or due to the biases which have gripped large sections of the law enforcement agencies. These agencies regard that only youth from one religious community are responsible for acts of terror. Khaitan also opines that putting forward the truth of such cases is also not of much use, as in such cases reports of honest investigations are overshadowed by the biased reporting and opinions in the print, TV, and social media. He is pinning his hopes on the judiciary and the people's campaigns for getting justice. The ongoing *dharana* in UP is drawing the attention of the social groups and is being sustained for over two weeks by the social activists and the pained and anguished community, whose young ones are being incarcerated and have to not only suffer the damage to their career prospects but have also to take the blame, which ostracizes them from social life. In this direction, various efforts have been undertaken in the past, but after temporary response and restraint, the investigation agencies lapse into their usual prejudiced actions.

This can not only be seen in the case of UP, but overall in the wide gulf between the promises and actual actions of the so-called secular parties. While in Maharashtra the Congress coalition came to power with the promise of implementing the Shrikrishna Commission report of 1992–1993 riots, after coming to power on this promise, it put forward the usual excuses and the guilty police officers and political leadership continued to be in their positions of power despite sufficient proof of their involvement in instigating and participating in the riots. As far as justice to the victims and action against the guilty is concerned, the Samajwadi Party seems to be no different. The R.D. Nimesh Commission has provided the full truth based on which it can proceed to punish the guilty police officers, but that is what is being avoided. The credentials of so-called secular parties are more or less similar, be it Congress or the Samajwadi Party; they have a very opportunistic attitude as far as the justice toward minorities is concerned. While communal parties are out to do away with the rights of minorities and deny them justice through and through, these so-called secular parties have dual character. They promise and are unable to deliver as their calculations are built around the vote bank politics.

This is due to multiple factors. One is that these supposedly secular parties are also being trapped by considerations other than the values of secularism. So, controlling communal violence, which is possible if there is adequate determination to do so, is not being done effectively. The second reason is the communalized state machinery, the investigating agencies, the police, and the bureaucracy. How to investigate the cases and how to frame the innocents is an easy enough job, which the authorities do, and their khaki uniform empowers them to do it with ease. It is precisely due to this that the fate of inquiry commission reports has not been a significant one. Starting from the Madon Commission of inquiry into the Bhiwandi riots, to the Shrikrishna Commission and the Liberhan Commission reports, the outcome, taking action based on the report, is close to zero, as the implementing authorities, and political leadership, are opportunists and lack the strength to stick to principles.

So where do we go from here? While the communal forces are out to proactively browbeat the religious minorities, the secular formations do not have the backbone to ensure justice and equity. It is here that the social activism which has prominently come up during the last two decades in particular needs to be strengthened. The activist groups have taken up these issues seriously and the initiatives by social activists are a major landmark in this direction. One wonders why the left parties, which should be principally secular to the core, are shunning these efforts. Their joining these efforts to get equity and justice for minorities will put pressure on parties like Congress and the Samajwadi Party to try to become sincere in their efforts.

The efforts through the judiciary and popular protests have to be intensified. The rot set in our democratic polity due to the infiltration of communalism through different mechanisms is very dangerous to the values of our constitution. It is time that we as a nation introspect and get over the biases and prejudiced behavior toward the weaker sections of our society. The path to social progress is paved through amity and justice. Professional attitude in the investigation of acts of violence, communal amity, and justice for all are the prerequisites of social progress, the progress of society in the real sense.

Appendix G: *A Moment of Silence* (by Emmanuel Ortiz)

Before I start this poem, I'd like to ask you to join me in a moment of silence in honor of those who died in the World Trade Center and the Pentagon last September 11th.

I would also like to ask you to offer up a moment of silence for all of those who have been harassed, imprisoned, disappeared, tortured, raped, or killed in retaliation for those strikes, for the victims in both Afghanistan and the U.S.

And if I could just add one more thing...

A full day of silence for the tens of thousands of Palestinians who have died at the hands of U.S.-backed Israeli forces over decades of occupation.

Six months of silence for the million and-a-half Iraqi people, mostly children, who have died of malnourishment or starvation as a result of an 11-year U.S. embargo against the country.

Before I begin this poem, two months of silence for the Blacks under Apartheid in South Africa, where homeland security made them aliens in their own country.

Nine months of silence for the dead in Hiroshima and Nagasaki, where death rained down and peeled back every layer of concrete, steel, earth and skin and the survivors went on as if alive.

A year of silence for the millions of dead in Viet Nam-a people, not a war-for those who know a thing or two about the scent of burning fuel, their relatives' bones buried in it, their babies born of it.

A year of silence for the dead in Cambodia and Laos, victims of a secret war ... ssssshhhhh .... Say nothing ... we don't want them to learn that they are dead.

Two months of silence for the decades of dead in Colombia, whose names, like the corpses they once represented, have piled up and slipped off our tongues.

Before I begin this poem,
An hour of silence for El Salvador...
An afternoon of silence for Nicaragua...
Two days of silence for the Guetmaltecos...
None of whom ever knew a moment of peace in their living years.
45 seconds of silence for the 45 dead at Acteal, Chiapas
25 years of silence for the hundred million Africans who found their graves
far deeper in the ocean than any building could poke into the sky.
There will be no DNA testing or dental records to identify their remains.
And for those who were strung and swung from the heights of sycamore trees
in the south, the north, the east, the west ... 100 years of silence ...

For the hundreds of millions of indigenous peoples from this half of right here,
Whose land and lives were stolen,
In postcard-perfect plots like Pine Ridge, Wounded Knee, Sand Creek, Fallen
Timbers, or the Trail of Tears.
Names now reduced to innocuous magnetic poetry on the refrigerator of our
consciousness ...

So you want a moment of silence?
And we are all left speechless
Our tongues snatched from our mouths
Our eyes stapled shut

A moment of silence
And the poets have all been laid to rest
The drums disintegrating into dust

Before I begin this poem,
You want a moment of silence
You mourn now as if the world will never be the same

And the rest of us hope to hell it won't be.
Not like it always has been

Because this is not a 9-1-1 poem
This is a 9/10 poem,
It is a 9/9 poem,
A 9/8 poem,
A 9/7 poem

This is a 1492 poem.
This is a poem about what causes poems like this to be written

And if this is a 9/11 poem, then
This is a September 11th poem for Chile, 1971
This is a September 12th poem for Steven Biko in South Africa, 1977
This is a September 13th poem for the brothers at Attica Prison, New York,
1971.

This is a September 14th poem for Somalia, 1992.
This is a poem for every date that falls to the ground in ashes
This is a poem for the 110 stories that were never told
The 110 stories that history chose not to write in textbooks
The 110 stories that that CNN, BBC, The New York Times, and Newsweek
ignored
This is a poem for interrupting this program.

And still you want a moment of silence for your dead?
We could give you lifetimes of empty:
The unmarked graves
The lost languages
The uprooted trees and histories
The dead stares on the faces of nameless children

Before I start this poem we could be silent forever
Or just long enough to hunger,
For the dust to bury us
And you would still ask us
For more of our silence.

If you want a moment of silence
Then stop the oil pumps
Turn off the engines and the televisions
Sink the cruise ships
Crash the stock markets
Unplug the marquee lights,
Delete the instant messages,
Derail the trains, the light rail transit
If you want a moment of silence, put a brick through the window of Taco
Bell,
And pay the workers for wages lost
Tear down the liquor stores,
The townhouses, the White Houses, the jailhouses, the Penthouses and the
Playboys.

If you want a moment of silence,
Then take it
On Super Bowl Sunday,
The Fourth of July
During Dayton's 13 hour sale
Or the next time your white guilt fills the room where my beautiful people
have gathered

You want a moment of silence
Then take it
Now,
Before this poem begins.
Here, in the echo of my voice,
In the pause between goosesteps of the second hand

In the space between bodies in embrace,
Here is your silence
Take it.
But take it all
Don't cut in line.
Let your silence begin at the beginning of crime.

But we,
Tonight we will keep right on singing
For our dead.
—Emmanuel Ortiz, November 11, 2002

This poem was forwarded to SeeingBlack.com by poet Sharan Strange. February 4, 2003. (http://www.seeingblack.com/2003/x020403/ poetry_feb.shtml#ortiz [last accessed on August 28, 2014]).

Bibliography

ABC News Special Report. "Planes Crash into World Trade Center," 8.35 AM ET, Tuesday, September 11, 2001 (http://emperors-clothes.com/9-11backups/abc911.htm [last accessed on August 28, 2014]).

Ahmad, Aijaz. *Iraq, Afghanistan & the Imperialism of Our Time*. Delhi: Left Word Books, 2004.

————. *On Communalism & Globalization: Offensives of the Far Right*. Gurgaon, Haryana: Three Essays Collective, 2003.

Ahmed, Nafees Mosaddeq. *The War on Freedom*. New York: Media Monitor Networks, 2002.

Akbar, M.J. *The Shade of Sword*. Delhi: Roli Books, 2002.

Ali, Tariq. *Military Rule or People's Power*. London: Jonathan Cape, 1970.

————. "Questions and Answers on War in Afghanistan," October 6, 2001 (http://www.counterpunch.org/2001/10/06/questions-and-answers-about-war-in-afghanistan/ [last accessed on August 28, 2014]).

————. *The Clash of Fundamentalism: Crusades, Jihads & Modernity*. Delhi: Rupa, 2003.

Andreas, Joel. *Addicted to War*. Kolkata: Earthcare Books, 2004.

Armstrong, Karen. *Islam: A Short History*. New York: Modern Library, 2002 (http://www.equip.org/articles/islam-a-short-history/ [last accessed on August 28, 2014]).

————. *Muhammad: A Biography of the Prophet*. London: Weidenfeld & Nicolson History, 2001.

Asfahani, Imam Raghib. *Mufradat al-Qur'an*. Lahore, 1971.

Baweja, Harinder (ed.). *26/11 Mumbai Attacked*. New Delhi: Lotus Collection, 2009.

Research Unit for Political Economy. "Behind the Invasion of Iraq." *Aspects of Indian Economy*, no. 33–34. Mumbai, 2002.

Bonner, Arthur. *Democracy in India: A Hollow Shell*. Washington: The American University Press, 1994.

Bose, Arun. *India's Social Crisis*. Delhi: Oxford University Press, 1985.

Chomsky, Noam. *Turning the Tide*. Boston: South End Press, 1985 (http://www.campusactivism.org/akreider/essays/res3.txt [last accessed on August 28, 2014]).

————. *Pirates and Emperors, International Terrorism in the Real World*. New York: Clairmont Research and Publication, 1986, 3.

Chossudovsky, Michel. "Who Is Osama bin Laden?" Centre for Research on Globalisation (CRG), Montréal, 2001 (http://globalresearch.ca/articles/CHO109C.html [last accessed on August 28, 2014]).

Christopher, Jaffrelot. "Hindu Nationalism: Strategies in Ideology Building." *Economic and Political Weekly,* March 20, 1993, 517–524.

Cogswell, David. *Chomsky for Beginners.* Hyderabad: Orient Longman, 1996.

Cooley, John. *Unholy Wars: Afghanistan, America, and International Terrorism.* London: Pluto Press, 2002.

Dev, Arjun. *Story of Civilization,* Vol. I. Delhi: NCERT, 1999.

Dhavan, Rajeev. "Get the Guilty." *Times of India,* August 23, 2006.

Douglas, Heynes and Gyanbv Prakash (eds). *Contesting Power: Resistance and Everyday Racial Relations in South Asia.* Delhi: Oxford University Press, 1991, 6.

Durran, Khalid. "The Globalization of Terrorism." In *Review,* Fall 2000.

Engineer, Asghar Ali. "Concept of Islamic State." *Aman,* April–May 1999.

———. *Origin and Development of Islam.* Hyderabad: Orient Longman, 1987.

———. *Islam and Modern Age,* Vol. I. Mumbai: Institue of Islamic Studies, 1998.

———. *Islam and the Concept of Jihad,* Vol. I. Mumbai: Institute of Islamic Studies, 1998.

———. *The Islamic State.* Delhi: Vikas, 1994.

Esposito, John L. and John O. Voll. *Islam and Democracy.* New York: Oxford University Press, 1996.

Gardezi, Hasan N. "A Brief History of Islamic State of Pakistan." *Indian Journal of Secularism,* October 2001, 35.

Gatade, Subhash. *Godse's Children.* Delhi: Pharos Media, 2011.

Grare, F. *Political Islam in the Indian Subcontinent.* New Delhi: Manohar, 2001.

Grunebaum, G.E. von, Wiesbaden: OTTO Harassowitz. The Beginnings of Islamic Theology. In *The Cultural Context of Medieval Learning.* Murdoch, J.E., Sylla, E.D. (eds). New York: Springer, 1970.

Hasan, Mushirul. Interview. "The Attack will Sensitise Americans Towards the World Outside the US." In Ram Puniyani (ed.) *Terrorism, Imperialism and War.* BUILD, 2002.

Hensman, Rohini. *Terrorism, Imperialism and War.* Mumbai: Build, 2002.

Hinnells, John, and Eric Sharpe (eds). *Hinduism.* New Caste: Oriental Press, 1972, 128.

Hiro, Dilip. *Islamic Fundamentalism.* London: Paladin, 1988.

Hoodbhoy, Pervez. "The Genesis of Global Jihad in Afghanistan," revised version. Paper presented in the Civil War and Cold War, 1975–1990, Institute of African Studies, Columbia University, New York, NY, November 14–15, 2002, mimeographed.

Hourani, A. *Arabic Thought in the Liberal Age 1798–1939.* London: Oxford University Press, 1962.

Huntington, Samuel. *Clash of Civilizations and the Remaking of World Order.* New York: Simon and Schuster, 1996.

Imam, Zafar. *Iraq-2003: The Return of Imperialism.* Delhi: Aakar Books, 2004, 112.

Judelson, Catherine. *Dictionary for Believers and Non-Believers.* Moscow: Progress Publishers, 1989.

Karan, Vijay. *War by Stealth, Terrorism in India,* New Delhi: Viking, 1997.

Khairnar, Suresh, Ahmad Kadar, and Arvind Ghosh. *Malegaon to Ajmer, Trail of Terror.* edited by Ram Puniyani. All India Secular Forum, 2010.

Khan, Q. *Al-Mawardi's Theory of State.* Lahore: Bazm-I Iqbal, 1983.

Kupferberg, Chaim. "The Propaganda Preparation for 9/11," June 13, 2002 (http://www.globalresearch.ca/articles/KUP206A.html [last accessed on August 28, 2014]).

Koshy, Ninan. *War on Terror: Reordering the World.* Delhi: Left Word, 2002.

Leibowitz, Yeshayahu. "The Territories." *Yediot,* April 1968, reprinted in *Ha'aretz,* March 16, 1969.

Lokshahi Hakk Sangathan. The assault on Afghanistan and the real intent behind it, Mumbai 2001.

Maley, William. *Afghanistan & the Taliban: The Rebirth of Fundamentalism?* Delhi: Penguin Books India, 2001, 253.

Mamdani, Mahmood. *Good Muslim Bad Muslim.* Hyderabad: Orient Longman, 2003.

———. *Good Muslim: Bad Muslim.* Delhi: Permanent Black, 2005.

Manfred, A.Z. *A Short History of the World.* Moscow: Progress Publishers, 1974.

Mansfield, Peter. *The Arabs.* Harmondsworth: Penguin Books, 1978.

McCoy, Alfred. "Drug Fallout: The CIA's Forty Year Complicity in Narcotics Trade." *The Progressive,* August 1, 1997.

Mehta, Vinod. "Ah Bombay."*Outlook,* December 8, 2008.

Miller, Roland E. *Muslim Friends.* Hyderabad: Orient Longman, 2000.

Murlidharan, Sukumar. *America's War. Frontline,* September 29–October 12, 2001.

Murshed, Zubair. "A Muslim Malaise." *Pakistan Today,* August 8, 2013.

Mushrif, S.M. *Who Killed Karkare: The Real Face of Terrorism in India.* New Delhi: Pharos Media, 2010.

Nehru, Jawaharlal. *The Discovery of India.* New York: John Day, 1946, 66.

Noorani, A.G. *Islam and Jihad.* Delhi: LeftWord, 2002.

Omvedt, Gail. *Dalit Visions (Tract for the Times—8).* New Delhi: Orient Longman, 1995, 7–12.

Prashad, Vijay. *War against the Planet: The Fifth Afghan War, Imperialism, & Other Assorted Fundamentalisms.* Delhi: LeftWord, 2002, 110.

Puniyani, Ram. *Communal Politics.* Delhi: SAGE, 2002.

———. *Fascism of Sangh Parivar.* Trivandrum: Mythri Publishers, 2001.

Puniyani, Ram. *Mumbai Post 26/11*. Edited by Hashmi Shabnam. Delhi: SAGE, 2009.

———. *Terrorism, Imperialism and War*. Mumbai: Build, 2002.

———. *Terrorism: Perceptions versus Reality*. Trivandrum: Mythri, 2010, 15.

Rashid, Ahmad. *Taliban: Militant Islam, Oil and Fundamentalism in Central Asia*. New Haven, CT: Yale University Press, 2000.

Reghunath, Leena Gita. "The Believer: Swami Aseemanand's Radical Service to the Sangh." *Caravan Magazine*, February 1, 2014.

Reinhart, Tanya. *Israel Palestine*. Delhi: Left Word, 2003.

Rodinson, Maxim. *Islam and Capitalism*. London: Allen Lane, 1974.

Roy, Arundhati. *The Algebra Of Infinite Justice*. India: Flamingo, 2002.

Roy, Oliver. *The Failure of Political Islam*. London: I.B. Tauris, 1994.

Ruppert, Michael C. "The Lie Won't Stand, Bush Administration Explanations for Pre-9-11 Warnings Fail the Test." May 16, 2002, The Wilderness website: http://www.fromthewilderness.com/free/ww3/051602_liewontstand.html (see also http://www.tenc.net/, IllarionBykov and Jared Israel [last accessed on August 28, 2014]).

Rutenburg, Victor (ed.). *Feudal Society and Its Culture*. Moscow: Progress Publishers, 1988.

Said, Edward. *Peace and Its Discontents*. London: Vintage, 1995, xxi.

Said, Edward W. *The End of the Peace Process: Oslo & After*. New York: Vintage Books, 2000, 389.

Sanghavi, Vir. *26/11: The Attack on Mumbai*. Gurgaon, Haryana: Penguin Books India, 2009.

Savarkar, V.D. *Hindutva*. Nagpur: Suruchi Prakashan, 1923, 94.

Schmitt, Eric. "U.S. Plan for Iraq is Said to Include Attack on 3 Sides". *New York Times*, July 5, 2002.

Sebastian, Thomas. *War against People*. Mumbai: J&P Publishers and Distributors, 2002.

Sharma, Geetesh. *Dharma ke Naam Par*. Delhi: Rajkamal Prakashan, 2003.

Simpson, Alan, and Glen Ranwala. "The Dishonest Case for War on Iraq." Labor against the War, Counter-Dossier, September 2002.

Suri, Sanjay. "The Great Britain Bust." *Outlook*, August 28, 2006.

Tansey, Stephen. *Politics*. London: Routledge, 2000.

Thapar, Romila. *Early India*. Delhi: Penguin, 2002.

———. "Syndicated Moksha?." *Seminar*, 1987, 14–22.

Tokarey, S. *History of Religion*. Moscow: Progress Publishers, 1986.

Tripathi, Arun, et al. *Muslim Atankwad Banam America*. Delhi: Vani Prakashan, 2002.

Zakaria, Farid. "The Roots of Rage." *Newsweek Weekly*, Washington, October 12, 2001.

Index

About the Author

Ram Puniyani is currently the Chairman at the Center for Study of Society and Secularism, Mumbai. He was a Professor of Biomedical Engineering, IIT Mumbai, and took voluntary retirement in 2004, and is currently working for communal harmony. He has been involved with human rights activities for the past two decades. He has also involved himself with groups working for workers' rights. Ram Puniyani is also associated with various secular and democratic initiatives, namely, All India Secular Forum, Center for Study of Society and Secularism, and Anhad.